THE MODERN RAF

THE ROYAL AIRFORCE INTO THE 21ST CENTURY

Peter G Dancy

Royal Air Force
BREVETS

PILOT

NAVIGATOR

AIR ENGINEER

FIGHTER CONTROLLER
(Airborne)

AIR ELECTRONICS
OPERATOR

AIR TECHNICIAN

AIR LOADMASTER

PARACHUTE JUMPING
INSTRUCTOR
(Honorary Aircrew)

AIR QUARTERMASTER
(Obsolete)

AIR OBSERVER
(Obsolete)

AIR SIGNALLER
(Obsolete)

FLIGHT ENGINEER
(Obsolete)

BOMB AIMER
(Obsolete)

OBSERVER RADIO
(Obsolete)

AIR GUNNER
(Obsolete)

WIRELESS OPERATOR

MET AIR OBSERVER

Command and Group Badges

SWIFT TO ATTACK

VINCEMUS

NIET ZONDER ARBYT

Contents

Introduction
Addendum

Strike Command
No. 1 Group - Squadrons - Roles - Badges & Markings
No. 2 Group   ..   ..
No. 3 Group   ..   ..

Personnel and Training Command (Flying Training Schools and OCUs)

Looking to the Future

Appendix I :   Order of Battle
Appendix II: Basic Data - Airplanes
Appendix III: National Markings (introduction of)

Bombardier Global Express (ZJ690) the RAF (ASTOR) Battlefield Surveillance airplane

Note: ASTOR airplanes are to be based at RAF Waddington, Lincs, from 2005.

Copyright ©2003 Peter G Dancey

ISBN 0-946995-70-2

Published by **Galago Books** 42 Palace Grove, Bromley, Kent BR1 3HB England

Introduction

Throughout its life the RAF's power and strength has been expressed by the squadrons, flights, and special units and the personnel that man them, along with the support of its training and operational conversion units. Throughout its existence the RAF's strength has risen and fallen in line with the requirements and budgetary constraints of the day. As we move into the 21st Century the service sees itself struggling to meet its world-wide commitments. Equipped with a minimum of squadron's and aircraft, many of which are often on repair, in-depth service, or upgrade modernisation programmes, often less than 50% of its inventory is available for front-line operations. During the two great wars the RFC and latterly the RAF built up rapidly to peaks of strength, but at other times were allowed to fall back to dangerously low levels. Certainly even today if it were not for the tenacity and foresight of senior air force staff at the Air Ministry, in allocating Flying Training School's (FTS) and Operational Conversion Units (OCUs), reserve squadron status, many would have faded into oblivion and the modern day air force would have an even greatly depleted battle order.

Over the years hundreds of squadrons have been formed fulfilling a variety of roles. Including, interception, air defence, fighting, bombing, attack, reconnaissance, transport, general purpose, communications, liaison, special duties and many others. Often each of these units have long and exciting histories and stories to tell, with each one worthy of a book in its own right. Indeed many have. It is the purpose of this book to provide a pictorial review of the modern day battle order.

Currently operations are being undertaken by Royal Air Force units world-wide, reflecting the standing of the service and the interests of the United Kingdom in the new world order and the coalitions on-going fight against terrorism. It is now more than a decade since the Berlin Wall was torn down, with the promise of everlasting peace and a better future. The initial euphoria was short lived, and in truth the world is now a much more uncertain place in which to live. In the last decade alone, the RAF has been called on to deploy its operational squadrons to the Gulf, the Balkans, the former Republic of Yugoslavia, Kosovo, and in Africa. Wherever national interests or those of our friends and allies have been at stake, the RAF has been called upon. It has deployed its air power with great speed, flexibility and concentration of effort in often less than desirable conditions for its ever willing air and ground crews. All this at a time when increasing financial constraints and budgetary reviews made it increasingly difficult to deliver air power as and when needed in a cost effective manner with the resources available. Nevertheless, leaner and fitter after drastic rationalisation and re-organisation, the Royal Air Force is ready to face the challenges of air warfare in the 21st Century. The squadrons remaining in the modern battle order truly representative and ably equipped to carry forward the true traditions of the service.

Peter G. Dancey
MK 2002

Acknowledgements :-
My sincere thanks goes to the Air Historical Branch, MoD (Air), BAE Systems (formerly BAe), Public Records Office Kew, RAF Museum Hendon and many other sources that have assisted with the compilation and verification of facts and figures and historical details.

Photographs:-   T. Shia (first published Air Power International - various editions)
                BAE Systems (formerly BAe), MoD, RAF, and authors collection.

Addendum

At the time this book was in its final preparation, elements of the following operational units were deployed to the Gulf, in case of military action against Iraq. Initial deployments were estimated to be in excess of one hundred aircraft and twenty-seven helicopters. In-theatre Composite squadrons to be based at airfields in Kuwait, Oman, Saudi Arabia and Turkey.

Elements and equipment were drawn from the following squadrons:

Nos 8 and 23 Squadrons - Boeing E-3 Sentry AWACS command and control planes

Nos 12, 14, 31 and 617 Squadrons - Panavia Tornado GR4 strike bombers equipped to carry Paveway precision-guided bombs.

Nos 2 and 13 Squadrons - Panavia Tornado GR4A reconnaissance planes

Nos 11, 25, 43 and 111 Squadrons - Panavia Tornado F-3 Air Defence fighters, upgraded variants with ASRAAM (Advanced Short-Range Air-to-Air Missiles).

Nos 6, 41, and 54 Squadrons - Sepecat Jaguar GR 3A ground-attack and reconnaissance planes

Nos 1 and 3 Squadrons - BAe/MDC Harrier GR 7 ground attack/close air support planes equipped to carry US-made Maverick anti-tank missiles.

Nos 10 and 101 Squadrons - BAC VC-10 transport/tanker-transports

Nos 24, 30, 47 and 70 Squadrons - Lockheed Hercules C-130H and C-130J tactical transport planes

Nos 99 Squadron - Boeing C-17 Globemaster III strategic transports.

Nos 7, 18 and 27 Squadrons - Boeing-Vertol CH-47 Chinook and Puma HC-1 helicopters.

RAF Regiment: Nos 1, 2, 16, 34 and 51 Squadrons for airfield defence.

In addition:-

BAe/HS Nimrod MR 2s (**Kinloss Wing**) and Nimrod R1 (**No. 51 Squadron**) and EE Canberra PR 9 (**No. 39 Squadron**) reconnaissance and electronic warfare airplanes, and Chinooks (**JHC**) equipped for special forces operations.

Strike Command. H.Q. RAF High Wycombe, Buckinghamshire.

Strike Command was formed on 30 April 1968, by merging Fighter and Bomber Commands and later Transport and Coastal Command. The Command is also an essential part of the NATO organisation.

The Air Ministry reporting to the Ministry of Defence, London, has two RAF Commands reporting to it: 1. Strike Command 2. Personnel and Training Command. Strike Command is by far the most important being responsible for all operational Groups and detachments. Units under the auspices of Strike Command are:

No. 1 Group comprising :- Canberra, Hawk, Tornado, Harrier, Jaguar and Eurofighter, to enter service 2005. Tactical and Offensive Support Helicopters (Joint Helicopter Command - under Army control)

No. 2 Group ..   ..   Transport C-17, C-130/J, Air Refuelling, Strategic Recce, E-3D Sentry (AWACS), Battlefield surveillance : Bombardier Global Express (ASTOR), & No. 32 (Royal) Squadron

No. 3 Group ..   ..   Nimrod, SAR Helicopters, Harrier/Sea Harrier Joint Force 2000 (later renamed as Joint Force Harrier)

Additional responsibilities are RAF Cyprus; RAF Mount Pleasant, Falkland Islands; Dahran, Saudi Arabia, Muharraq, Bahrain; Incirlik, Turkey; and the Tornado IDS detachment at Ali Al Salem, AB Kuwait.

Strike Command with its headquarters buried in the English countryside high on the hill at High Wycombe, Bucks, is responsible for all the RAF's front-line squadrons both at home and overseas. As its name implies Strike Command has the primary responsibility for tactical strike, attack, and offensive support units. It is also tasked with air intercept missions in defence of the realm and other important duties including airlift, air sea rescue, airborne early warning, in-flight refuelling, VIP transport - No. 32 (Royal) Squadron, maritime and photographic operations, and soon, with the arrival of five specially modified Bombardier Global Express short-haul airliners, battlefield surveillance.

The back-bone of the Command's offensive capability is provided by the Panavia Tornado both in its Interdictor Strike (IDS) and Air Defence Variant (ADV) with its powerful GEC/Ferranti A.I. 24 intercept radar. Offensive support being the premise of the BAe/MDC Harrier GR 7 and Sepecat Jaguar GR.3/3A airplanes. While it is true these airplanes are all thirty year old designs, excepting for the the Tornado ADV variant soon to undergo it own update programme, they all are highly enhanced variants bearing little resemblance to their Mk I counterparts. Indeed continued development and upgrade has produced virtually 'new' airplanes with most likely to remain in service for the next two decades or more. Until deliveries of the ninety or so Lockheed Martin F-35 (JSF) Joint Strike fighters on order, are made. The RAF's premier combat plane for the 21st Century is to be the Eurofighter Typhoon, a light-weight interceptor and multi-role combat plane, like the Panavia Tornado and Sepecat Jaguar, another joint venture involving other European partners. The UK's current requirement standing at 250 airplanes to include thirty-seven 2-seaters. Options exist for an additional 58 with a possible further 70 as Harrier GR 7/9 replacements. Total RAF procurement could exceed 350 airplanes... Although currently (mid-2002), industry sources suggest the overall procurement will be reduced by about 80 airplanes...

No. 1 GROUP

Badge : A black panther's head erased.
Motto : "Swift to attack"
Authority : King George VI, June, 1941

No. 1 Group's badge commemorates the code-name "Panther" which the Group had in 1939, at the time of its mobilisation for service in France as the Advanced Air Striking Force. No. 1 Group is the largest of the three Strike Command Groups assigned 25 squadrons and 6 Operational Conversion Units (OCUs) and overseas units, 50% of the 21st Century battle order...

The three primary combat types consist of the Panavia Tornado, BAe/MDC Harrier, and the Sepecat Jaguar airplanes. No. 1 Group (Bomber) was originally formed at RAF Abingdon, Oxon, on 1 May 1936. Disbanded on 22 December 1939, it reformed on 22 June 1940, by renaming the Advanced Air Strike Force H.Q. at Hucknall. On 1 November 1967, No. 1 Group merged with No. 3 Group, the combined unit assuming the No. 1 Group mantle. Transferred to the new Strike Command on 30 April 1968.

Inventory (includes Reserve (R) Squadrons - OCUs) :
Panavia Tornado GR 4/4A (142) — Nos. II, 9, 12, 13, 14, 15(R), 31, and 617 Squadrons
Panavia Tornado F. 3 (98) (89 operational) — Nos. 11, 25, 43, 56(R), and 111
BAe Hawk T1 (5) T1A (12) — No. 100 Squadron
Eurofighter Typhoon (232) — on order
BAe/MDC Harrier GR 7/T.10   (62) — Nos. 1, 3, IV, and 20(R) Squadrons
Sepecat Jaguar GR3/3A/T.2B (60) — Nos 6, 16(R), 41, and 54 Squadrons
Boeing Vertol Chinook HC 2/2A//3 (53)— Nos 7, 18, 27 (JHC) and 78 Squadron
Westland Puma HC 1   (32)—   Nos 33 and 230 Squadrons (JHC)
Westland Merlin HC 3   (22)— No. 28 Squadron (18 HC 3 allocated to squadron) (JHC)
Westland Wessex HC 2C (3) — No. 84 Squadron

Strike/Attack:
Since it entered service in January 1982, the Mach 2.2 Panavia Tornado IDS (InterDictor Strike) plane has been at the forefront of the RAF's strike attack force. 229 IDS variants were delivered to form eleven operational front-line squadrons tasked with overland strike/attack and reconnaissance.

Eight were based in Germany, with a dual conventional and nuclear tasking, and were divided between RAF Bruggen and RAF Laarbruch. They were assigned to the 2nd Tactical Air Force, supporting the NATO Central Army Group. Currently all Tornado units have been withdrawn from German soil, although it was announced in 2000 that consideration was being given to joint operation of RAF GR 4/4A (110) with German Air Force IDS variants (220). The UK-based Tornado squadrons were tasked with a more strike-orientated role and two, Nos. 12 and 617 Squadrons with GR 1B airplanes were later tasked with maritime strike duties on retirement of the Blackburn Buccaneer low-level maritime strike bombers, although now maritime ASUW (Anti-Surface Unit Warfare), accounted for only 40% of their tasking. The remaining 60% was concerned with the standard GR 1 overland role. All were available to the SACEUR's (Supreme Allied Commander Europe) Strategic Reserve (Air). Currently with the withdrawal of the Sea Eagle missile from use in 2001, both the former maritime strike squadrons airplanes are being upgraded to GR 4 standard for the units to assume the normal overland strike role. Modifications include a new BAe Systems Electronic Warfare Defence System, Forward Looking Infra-Red (FLIR), Global Positioning System (GPS), digital map technology, a new pilots Head Up Display (HUD) and an updated weapons control system. Each GR 4 airplane will be able to carry its own laser designation pod for 'smart weapon' deliver, the TIALD system which was first used in the Gulf War.

Unmarked TIALD-equipped No. 9 Squadron Tornado GR 4 receiving checks on a "wintry" flightline

(RAF)

A Panavia Tornado GR. IA taxies at Dharhan, March 1991, Gulf War

(RAF)

Panavia Tornado IDS (InterDictor Strike)

The Tri-national Tornado Training Establishment (TTTE) formed at RAF Cottesmore on 29 February 1981, was responsible for conversion training of Italian and Luftwaffe pilots and navigators as well as RAF aircrew, using German, Italian and British airplanes and instructors. At its peak the three training and one standards squadrons each had their own semi-official fin badge worn in addition to the unit's triangular 'TTTE' fin-top pennant. At the peak of operations the TTTE comprised 43 airplanes: RAF Tornado GR 1A (18), German Luftwaffe (19), Italian Air Force (6). Two former unit members are depicted below, Luftwaffe 45+91 and a member of the AMI. Subsequently the TTTE has ceased operations with each country now responsible for its own IDS Tornado conversion training. RAF Cottesmore, Rutland, is now home to the joint RN/RAF Harrier Strike Force 2000 (Joint Force Harrier).

Former TTTE Luftwaffe IDS Panavia Tornado

Former TTTE AMI IDS Panavia Tornado

No II (AC) Squadron

RAF Marham, Norfolk.   Strike/Recce
Tornado GR 4 /4A (12)
Motto : *Hereward*

No. 2

Formed at Farnborough on 13 May 1912, No. 2 Squadron RFC spent most of WW I on Western Front on army co-operation and reconnaissance duties, which is still its primary task today. It continued in the army co-operation role between the wars, flying as a tactical reconnaissance unit in WW II over France and the low countries, ending the war in Germany. Post-war the squadron remained in Germany, specialising in tactical reconnaissance, until the early 1990s, initially with Supermarine Swift FR. 5s, Hawker Hunter FR.10, MDC Phantoms, Sepecat Jaguars and then Panavia Tornado GR 1A fitted with the BAe 4000 infra-red linescan video camera system aft of the radar nose. Relocated to RAF Marham from Laarbruch in 1991, No. II (AC) Squadron operates the upgraded Tornado GR4/4A airplane in the same role.

Aircraft Markings and Codes
It was the squadron's B.E.2c airplanes that first carried unit markings, in April 1916, in the form of a triangle aft of the roundel. The triangle was black on clear doped aircraft and white others. The introduction of A.W. FK. 8 saw the introduction of a zig-zag stripe between the roundel and the tail-plane.
In the 1920s whilst based in Ireland the squadron's Bristol F 2b's carried two red stripes around the rear fuselage the space between them being filled by 'Flight' colours. White for "A" , Yellow for "B", and Blue for "C" Flight. The First World War black triangle marking re-appeared on the F 2b aircraft disappearing when the A.W. Atlas was introduced only to reappear again on the rear fuselage of the Audax with the aircraft serial superimposed on the triangle. On some of the later Audaxes the squadron badge was carried on the tail. The same marking were carried on Hawker Hectors the last pre-WW II airplane to remain all-silver.
Green/brown camouflage was introduced on the squadron's WW II Westland Lysanders with silver undersides and KO- unit codes. Replaced in 1941, by XV- which was used until 1943. Unit codes were not carried on No. 2 Squadron airplanes when it became part of the 2nd TAF until after the war when the new code OI- was used.
1951, brought the introduction of all-over silver Supermarine Spitfires, the same retained on the Meteor jets when introduced with the unit code "B" along with individual aircraft code letters. In 1952, the Meteors received camouflage retaining the codes until squadron markings and the famous triangle was resurrected. White on a black outline on each side of the fuselage roundel. These markings being retained throughout the Supermarine Swift and Hawker Hunter eras. Introduction of the FGR 2 Phantom saw the markings moved to the nose with the space between the triangles occupied by the Wake Knot. This being retained on Sepecat Jaguars and carried through to the Panavia Tornados in current use.

No. IX Squadron   RAF Marham, Norfolk.   Strike/Attack
                                        Tornado GR 4 (12)
                                        Motto : *Per noctum volamus* (Through the night we fly)

Formed on 8 December 1914, at St Omer, France, as a scouting unit from H.Q. Wireless Section., No. IXs early days on the Western Front, involved pioneering work on air-to-ground wireless trials, until concentrating on RFC bombing and reconnaissance tasks. It subsequently assumed the role of a night-bomber squadron and at the start of WW II was equipped with Vickers Wellington which was eventually replaced by the Avro Lancaster.

Post-war bombing operations has seen the squadron successively operate the Avro Lincoln, EE Canberra and the Avro Vulcan. No. IX was the first RAF unit to receive the Panavia Tornado GR 1 variant at RAF Honington in June, 1982, undertaking a wide range of detachments, trials work and deployments. The squadron's 'bat' badge was approved by H. R. H. King Edward VIII in November 1936, as the authorised version of an unofficial badge carried in 1927 on the squadron's Vickers Virginia night bombers. When based at Bruggen, the units HAS Complex was nicknamed 'Gotham City'.

Unofficial Badge

A former Avro Vulcan bomber operator, No IX Squadron became the worlds first front-line Tornado operator in June 1982. Four years later the squadron moved to Germany on 1 October 1986, and won the prestigious Salmond Trophy (awarded to RAF Germany squadrons for bombing and navigational accuracy) the same year. It followed this achievement with two second places successively in 1987 and 1988, before winning the trophy again in 1989. The squadron was nominated to become the first user of the BAe ALARM anti-radar missile. Following the Gulf War, on 1 January 1993, the squadron was formerly declared to NATO in the SEAD role. On the 2 November 1995, No IX Squadron was presented with the Wilkinson Battle of Britain Memorial Sword, in acknowledgement of its introduction and tactical development of ALARM. Subsequently the squadron was involved in operations in the Balkans operating from its base at Bruggen in Germany.

Aircraft Markings and Codes

No. IX Squadrons Tornadoes wear a green, yellow edged "bat" on the tail fin to signify its long wartime association with night bombing. On the nose is a green yellow outlined arrowhead on which the class C roundel is superimposed, see aircraft 'AL' overleaf. Individual aircraft lettering is suffixed with the unit letter "A". Also carried on the fin.

Unit markings were first introduced on No.IXs airplanes in April 1916, with a single broad band around the rear fuselage aft of the roundel, black on clear doped airplanes and white on Khaki drab machines. R .E. 8s "Harry Tates", were similarly marked although it is believed Bristol Fighters did not carry any unit markings.

The only markings on the silver-painted Vickers Vimy bombers was a "diving bird" badge on the nose, although when dark green (nivo) Vickers Virginias were received, a single numeral on the nose was carried. In 1927, names associated with Wessex were applied to aircraft with highlighted code letters. Handley Page Heyfords also had flight-coloured individual letters and trim on the wheel spats. Individual aircraft names were dropped. With the Vickers Wellington came night-bomber camouflage and the squadron code KA- painted aft of the fuselage roundel with an individual letter forward of the roundel. A large unit badge appeared on either side of the nose.

With the outbreak of WW II the official squadron code was changed to WS- and moved forward of the roundel on the port side. WS- was used throughout the war and post-war on Avro Lincoln bombers. The EE Canberras that followed carried more restrained markings, initially only a blue lightning flash on the nose. But, with the advent of the silver-painted Mk 6s a unit badge on the nose appeared also a grey-green "Bat", symbol surmounted with a yellow "IX" in red on the fin. Later light blue tip-tanks were used for a short while with some airplanes having a "9" flanked by Bats wings. Tail fins were also painted blue and had a white disc carrying a grey-green bat and Roman numerals IX in red or superimposed in yellow.

Avro Vulcan bomber marking varied considerably. By 1963, white-painted "anti-nuclear flash" aircraft had a large Bat symbol on the upper fin with a squadron badge between the fuselage roundel and the wing. With camouflaged Vulcans all such airplane markings disappeared. However, eventually at Waddington the station badge (City of Lincoln Arms) appeared on the fin along with a green Bat on a yellow disc. Since receiving Panavia Tornado strike planes unit markings have been as depicted. The squadrons Tornadoes wear the aircraft codes 'AA to 'AZ'

No. 9 Squadron Tornado

No. 12 Squadron

RAF Lossiemouth, Moray, Scotland, Strike/Attack
Tornado GR 4 (12)
Motto : Leads the field
Nickname "Flying Foxes"

Formed on 14 February 1915, at Netheravon, Wilts, during WW I, No. 12 Squadron flew almost exclusively on the Western Front in France. Its Fox emblem is believed to have been derived from the blood-sport of foxhunting, and the squadrons reputation for its daylight bombing development work. Subsequently, in the 1920s as the only RAF squadron to fly the superb Fairey Fox I bomber in its all-silver finish, it was the airplanes name to lend its association to the units badge. The unit is immortalised in RAF history by the Meuse Bridge attack in 1940, when two Victoria Crosses were awarded to the squadron. Since October, 1969, until the turn of the century when the Sea Eagle missile was withdrawn from use in 2001, the squadron has been associated with maritime attack tasks. Initially operating Blackburn Buccaneer maritime strike bombers, supplanted on 1 October 1993, by Tornado GR 1, when No 27 Squadron at Marham, took over the No.12 Squadron number-plate. Having converted to GR 1B Sea Eagle capable airplanes the squadron moved to Lossiemouth in Scotland on 7 January, 1994. Upgrade to Tornado GR 4 standard has seen No. 12 dedicated solely to the overland strike role, with the aircraft using the two letter code, starting "FA" ('F' for Fox in its badge).

Unofficial Badge

Aircraft Markings and codes
No. 12 Squadron airplanes carried no official markings until April 1916, when a single horizontal bar running, above the fuselage roundel from beneath the pilots seat to the tail was annotated, black on clear doped and white on Khaki drab B. E. 2c airplanes. The same marking was used on the squadrons B. E. 2e, but when R. E. 8s arrived in August 1917, a white strip along the lower longeron from the roundel to the rudder was substituted. All unit markings were removed in March 1918, but after the Armistice in November, 1918, the squadron started to paint large white Flight letters and numerals aft of the fuselage roundel.
The squadrons Airco D.H.9 bombers remained unmarked except for national insignia, but Fairey Fawns had a small black '12' in a circle high on the fin. Early Fairey Foxes used a similar unit symbol until the 'fox's mask' with a small Roman numeral 'XII' above it, was placed in the circle. The colour of the ring denoting the Flight, red for 'A', yellow for 'B' and blue for 'C'. By 1930, the number '12', was painted in black forward of the fuselage roundel in addition to the small fin marking, and this marking was retained on the squadron Hawker Harts and Hinds except during the 'Abyssinian' detachment. Later, camouflaged Fairey Battles also carried the numerals "12" until replaced by the official Air Ministry wartime code QE-, later changed to PH- , when war started. The PH- code was used throughout the war on the squadron's Vickers Wellington, Avro Lancaster and early Avro Lincoln airplanes, with an additional unit GZ- code allocated occasionally used on Lancasters. In 1952, all Avro Lincoln airplanes displayed enlarged serials instead of codes, No. 12 identifying itself by way of yellow airscrew spinners.

EE Canberras initially employed the Binbrook Wing 'flash' on the nose, painted in gold on No. 12 Squadron airplanes. On converting to B. 6 variants a 'leaping fox' was painted in red on the fin, but by 1958, the aircraft had green fins with the 'masked fox' emblem superimposed on a white disc. The nuclear weapon carrying Avro Vulcan IIs featured pale anti-flash national markings and the squadron 'Fox' markings on an over-all white finish, when the squadron first received the type, but camouflage schemes took over throughout Bomber command in 1964, as the low-level strike role was introduced. As all V-bomber units were now using the Central Servicing scheme at this time, no squadron markings were applied to any squadron airplanes at either RAF Coningsby or Cottesmore. Neither did the first of the squadron's Blackburn Buccaneer maritime strike bombers carry unit markings, although it was not long until the 'masked fox' emblem appeared on the sides of the engine intakes, usually on a white background. Later, individual identification letters were painted in black on the fin, changed to a two letter code when the squadron moved to Lossiemouth, with the letter 'F' preceding the airplane letter, both outlined in white. Later rather unusually the 'last three' of the airplanes serial was repeated in white on the fin, because the Spey engines exhaust smoke blackened the rear fuselage, often obscuring the full serial. Interestingly the 'last three' was also repeated in miniature on the inside of the airbrake doors, only visible of course, when they were open.

The squadron's dual-seat Hawker Hunter T 7 trainers carried similar markings. Although in contrast a No. 12 Squadron Hawker Hunter T.7 devoid of all unit markings, on a training mission is depicted overleaf. The last six operational Hawker Hunters in the RAF were all dual-seat T 7s based at Lossiemouth for training purposes with Nos. 12 and 208 Blackburn Buccaneer maritime strike squadrons.

RAF Panavia Tornado GR 4 model on BAe Systems stand at the Farnborough Air Salon

No. 13 Squadron

RAF   Marham, Norfolk, Strike/Tactical Recce.
Tornado GR4/4A (12)
Motto : *Adjuvamus tuendo* "We assist by watching"

Formed on 10 January 1915, No. 13 Squadron has operated predominantly on reconnaissance and army co-operation duties. Retained in the post-WW I battle order the squadron returned to the UK in March 1919, disbanding on 31 December that year. In April 1924, it reformed as an army co-operation unit. After serving in the UK and France in WW II it became a light-bomber unit operating in the Mediterranean. It remained in theatre post-war in the photo-recce role successively with D. H. Mosquito PR. 34, Meteor PR. 10, and EE Canberra PR. 7 and PR. 9 variants, returning to the UK in October 1978. The squadron disbanded in January 1982, reforming as the second Panavia Tornado GR 1A Squadron in November 1989. Today the squadron continues to operate the upgraded GR 4 variant, still in the strike recce role.

Aircraft markings and Codes.

The dagger was used as a squadron badge for some time, then a black Lynx's head was placed in front of the shield indicating vigilance. On reformation in 1924, no unit codes were carried. In January 1939, official AN- codes were issued, changing to OO- in September that year to be carried on Westland Lysander and Bristol Blenheim airplanes until November 1942. From which time no unit codes were carried until 1946.

Current Panavia Tornado markings are a dagger, a black Lynx's head affrontee on a white shield outlined in black at the top of the fin superimposed on a blue band outlined in yellow. Nose markings comprise a blue and green rectangle on each side of the roundel split by a yellow "lightning flash", the rectangle outlined in yellow.

On the flight-line four No. 13 Squadron GR 4s at readiness   (RAF)

12.

No. 14 Squadron   RAF Lossiemouth, Moray, Scotland. Strike (TIALD)
                                       Tornado GR 4 (12)
                                       Motto: I spread my wings and keep my promise (Arabic script)
                                       Nickname : "Crusaders"

No.14 Squadron formed at Shoreham, Sussex, on 3 February 1915, with B.E.2c and after a period of training left for the Middle East in November. From its bases in Egypt it provided support for the Army with its B.E.2s in Egypt, Palestine, the Western Desert and Arabia, including Lawrence's Arab revolt. Post WW I and throughout WW II the squadron served in the Middle East theatre on policing and bombing duties until 1945. In 1946, No. 14 Squadron returned to the European theatre at Wahn in Germany when No. 128 Squadron was renumbered No. 14 Squadron. Variously flying on fighter, light-bomber, and strike/attack duties.

No. 14 Squadron became the final RAF Germany Panavia Tornado unit when it re-equipped from the Sepecat Jaguar in October, 1985. The squadron has operated in the strike role for forty years, taking over the role with Canberras in 1962, and replacing these with MDC FGR Phantoms, in 1970, and then with Sepecat Jaguar GR 1 in 1975. Declared operational on Tornado on 1 November, 1985, No. 14 Squadron was the first of the RAF's Tornado units to receive the Hunting JP 233 airfield attack weapon. The squadrons crews played a prominent role within the Tabuk Tornado detachment during the Gulf War. In late 1993, the squadron received a substantial number of TIALD-capable airplanes from No. 617 Squadron who received Sea Eagle capable GR 1B airplanes for the now defunct maritime strike role. Subsequently the squadron has flown operations in the Balkans and seven hour strike missions in the 1999 Kosovo Conflict from its base at Bruggen in Germany. Albeit many of the Kosovo missions were aborted due to bad weather in line with NATO's policy to minimise collateral damage in the target area. The squadron's 'Crusader' badge and Arabic motto dates from the 1920s, when it was a Palestine-based light-bomber and army co-operation unit, stationed close the burial ground of St George.

Contasting desert-camouflages Tornado GR 1 fitted with ADV F.3 drop-tanks

Aircraft Markings and Codes

No squadron markings were carried in WW I, but the units Bristol Fighters had a broad black band painted around the fuselage aft of the roundel during the 1920s when on army co-operation duty. The squadron's Airco D.H. 9 day bombers carried an unofficial badge on the fin, but the Fairey IIIFs and Gordons had only large individual aircraft identification letters on the tail.

Unofficial Badge

No. 14

Somewhat surprisingly the camouflaged Vickers Wellesleys carried a squadron badge on the fin and large aircraft letters on the fuselage aft of the roundel. Bristol Blenheims and American Martin Marauders were emblazoned in similar manner - but without the badge.

WW II Wellington XIV bombers brought the official unit code CX- and the D. H. Mosquitos based in Scotland and latterly Germany, also carried this code. Unit and individual code letters of the airplanes of the 2nd TAF D. H. Mosquitos were yellow, outlined in black, and the squadron badge was carried on the fin. The squadron's ground-attack D. H. Vampires carried the Fassberg Wing 'lightning flash' on the nose and a squadron badge on a white disc on the fin. The D. H. Venom fighter-bombers had the badge superimposed on the nose 'flash', the 2nd TAF code letter 'B' aft of the fuselage boom roundels and the 'lightning flash' repeated on the tip tanks. Hawker Hunter day fighters were given the standard fighter style markings, a white rectangle with three blue diamonds superimposed, displayed on both each side of the fuselage roundel. Later Hunters had unit badges displayed on the nose and the airplanes letter in a black disc on the fin.

EE Canberra B(I)8s carried similar unit markings on the nose painted each side of the squadron badge, a version of the latter being painted on the fin. MDC FGR Phantoms used the same nose markings but carried the 'last three' digits of the airplanes serial in white on the upper portion of the fin. Sepecat Jaguar ground-attack planes carried the now famous 'fighter style' markings on the sides of the engine air intakes. Towards the end of the Phantom era the airplanes carried the unit code letter 'B' on the fin alongside the aircraft letter, both outlined in white.

Panavia Tornados carry similar identification markings, the 'Crusader' badge and white rectangles/blue diamonds on both sides of the fuselage below the pilot's cockpit, the squadron codes on the lower fin being outlined in silver, with a row of light blue diamonds first used on Hawker Hunter aircraft appear on the RWR fairing at the top of the fin. The squadron continues to use the code range 'BA' to 'BZ'.

No. 14 Squadron GR 1

No. 15(R) Squadron   RAF Lossiemouth, Moray, Scotland. (OCU) Tornado crew conversion
                                      Tornado GR 4/4A (26)
                                      Motto: Aim sure

After forming at South Farnborough, Hants, in March 1915, the squadron flew B.E. 2c and R.E. 8s on army co-operation tasks on the Western Front throughout the the remainder of the war. Post-war, after a period of test flying attached to the A&AEE at Martlesham Heath, Suffolk, the squadron assumed the bomber role in 1934, which it has retained ever since. Undertaking its full part in the bomber offensive of WW II variously flying, Fairey Battle Is, Bristol Blenheim IV, Vickers Wellington, Short Stirling and Avro Lancasters.

The squadron continued in the bomber role post-WW II, and after a short spell with Avro Lincoln, became one of the few units to use the Boeing B-29 Washington, which was operated in the interim pending delivery of the RAF's first jet bomber the EE Canberra in the latter half of the 1950s. As one of a number of units to operate the crescent-winged H. P. Victor, No. 15 Squadron eventually reformed in Germany during the late 1960s with the Blackburn Buccaneer strike bomber, conversion to Panavia Tornado GR. 1 began in July, 1983. The first RAF Germany unit to do so.

Following withdrawal from Laarbruch after the Gulf War in 1991, the squadron reformed at RAF Honington, Suffolk, with Tornado GR 1 taking over Tornado Tactical Weapons Conversion (TWCU) duties from No. 45 Squadron in June 1993, continuing in this role on re-locating to RAF Lossiemouth, Scotland in 1994. The demise of the TTTE (Tornado Tri-national Training Establishment) at Cottesmore has seen No. 15(R) Squadron assume the role of OCU for all current RAF IDS crews, a role in which it continues today with its upgraded GR4 mounts.

Aircraft markings and codes.

As with most RFC reconnaissance squadrons on the Western Front, no unit markings were carried until April 1916, when a single band, black on clear doped and white on khaki drab airplanes was painted around the fuselage immediately forward of the tailplane. In early 1918, the squadron's R. E. 8s were also carrying individual aircraft numerals aft of the fuselage roundel and also on the top decking behind the observer's cockpit. In March 1918, all unit markings were removed and were not displayed again until Hawker Harts were taken on charge in June 1934. These airplanes had the Roman numerals 'XV' forward of the fuselage roundel painted in red on 'A' Flight, yellow on 'B' Flight and blue on 'C' Flight airplanes. During the summer of the following year a small unit badge appeared on the Harts fin and similar markings were used on the Hinds that followed.

It is believed Fairey Battles carried the unique 'XV' marking until the official EF- code was issued after the Munich Crisis of 1938. EF- was carried to the rear of the fuselage roundel with an individual identification letter forward. In September 1939, the official code was changed to LS- and this was carried on all No. 15 squadrons airplanes until 1951, the only other unit distinguishing feature on some airplanes being a blue nose-wheel undercarriage door.

EE Canberra light-bomber based at Coningsby were distinctly anonymous, but on moving to Cottesmore in May 1954, a form of Station badge - a hunting horn and horseshoe - was painted in red on the fin, replaced at Honington by the Canberra Wing's 'pheasant' coloured white with red edging. As with most Canberra squadrons involved in the Suez Campaign, hurriedly applied yellow and black stripes were painted around the rear fuselage and across the wings for identification. Nuclear weapon carrying low-viz white painted H. P. Victor bombers had a small stylized version of the unit badge — a black Hind's head between yellow wings — on the upper portion of the fin, together with the 'XV' numerals. By 1962, all these markings were toned down in line with the airplanes national markings and serials and at the same time the Hind's head appeared in pale blue with black trim, pink wings and a pink 'XV', shadowed in pale blue.

The squadron's camouflaged Blackburn Buccaneers and Hunter T 7s used in Germany had 'XV' in white on the upper fin, these later being 'toned down' when repainted in red as low-viz markings became the norm in 1972. Although by 1974, the rules were relaxed slightly and the 'XV' returned more prominently displayed in white these markings retained on Panavia Tornados, that also carried a single black-painted identification letter on the fin. From 1984, this identification letter was preceded by the unit code letter 'E'.

No. 15 Squadron GR 1 in 'zoom' climb with full wing sweep

No. 31 Squadron

RAF Marham, Norfolk. Strike (SEAD)
Tornado GR 4 (12)
Motto : *In caelum indicum primus* — 'First into Indian skies'
Nickname : 'The Goldstars'

'A' Flight of the squadron formed in August 1915, at Farnborough, Hants, from part of No. 1 Reserve Squadron with B.E.2c (5). Leaving for India on 27 November 1915 arriving on 26 December 1915, the squadron was the first RAF unit to serve on the North West Frontier of India. At Nowshera, then Risalpur. 'B' Flight formed in February 1916, from part of No. 22 Squadron with B.E. 2c (6). 'C' Flight formed on 17 June, 1916, from 6th Brigade, Bombay. Following the Armistice the squadron remained in India on policing duties until WW II. By then it was a transport unit and later was to serve with distinction in the long campaign in Burma, flying Douglas Dakota over the 'Hump', engaged in troop-carrying and supply dropping.

Reformed post-war in the UK, the unit became the Metropolitan Communication Squadron at Hendon, north London, until becoming a tactical reconnaissance unit in Germany, with EE Canberra PR. 3 at Laarbruch in the 2nd TAF. In 1971, equipped with MDC Phantom FGR 2 its role changed to strike/attack and has remained so ever since. Having moved to RAF Bruggen, 'The Goldstars' became the first 'Bruggen Wing' Tornado squadron on 1 November 1984. The green and yellow chequers worn on the units Phantoms and Jaguars gave way to a green and yellow arrowhead and the traditional five-pointed star lost its traditional laurel wreath decoration.

Converting to Panavia Tornado GR 1 in 1984, like all the RAF Germany Tornado units the squadron's primary role was counter-air offensive and long-range interdiction, to strike at airfields and other targets behind enemy lines. The squadron soon showed its capabilities with its new mount, winning the Salmond Trophy in 1987. During the Gulf War, the unit provided the lead element of the Dhahran-based 'Composite' Squadron and also provided crews for the Muharraq detachment. Later the squadron became the second RAF unit capable of deploying the ALARM defence suppression missile. Along with its stable mates at Bruggen, No. 31 Squadron has been involved in the Balkan War and the Kosovo Conflict of 1999, flying long return bombing missions requiring in-flight refuelling from its then home base in Germany.

Aircraft Markings and Codes

No aircraft markings were carried on the squadrons airplanes in WW I, but some used letter/numeral identification during 1918-1919. When first received Bristol Fighters were similarly marked, using a single letter code aft of the roundel and the squadron number on the fin, but late in their careers a black band around the fuselage was used instead. Westland Wapitis also featured a single band together with an individual letter painted either on the rear or forward fuselage. Following authorisation of the unit badge a 'mullet' emblem appeared on the fin.

At first the squadron's Vickers Valentias were unmarked, except for individual code letters positioned aft of the fuselage roundel and repeated on the nose, but later some airplanes carried a name across the broad nose. In WW II No. 31 Squadron was allocated the code ZA-, although Douglas DC 2 and DC 3s were unmarked and the replacement C-47 Dakotas carried only individual aircraft letters.

When reformed post-war as the Metropolitan Communications Squadron, 'A' Flight used code CB- and 'B' Flight VS- with the Avro Anson C.12 and C.19 transports carrying the Transport Command diamond on the fin for a while. On returning to front-line operational flying the squadron painted the 'mullet' in yellow on a green disc on the fins of its Canberra PR. 7s and a squadron badge on the nose. These markings were retained on the MDC FGR 2 Phantoms, which also carried 'fighter-type' yellow and green markings on the nose. Sepecat Jaguars carried the same markings, but moved to the sides of the engine air intakes. Later towards the end of their tenure Jaguars had their individual code letter on the fin prefixed with the letter 'D' to denote the squadron. The squadrons Panavia Tornados introduced a new scheme, the squadron 'mullet' displayed on the fin with the two-letter identification code, and a yellow and green arrowhead painted around the nose roundel below the pilot's cockpit. The unit uses the 'DA to 'DZ' aircraft letter codes.

No 31 Squadron IDS GR.1 Panavia Tornado shows off its full load of stores

No. 31 Squadron Tornado

No. 617 Squadron

RAF   Lossiemouth, Moray, Scotland, Strike/Attack
Tornado GR 4 (12)
Motto :   *Apres moi, le deluge* - 'After me, the flood'
Nickname :   'The Dambusters'

The infamous No. 617 'Dambusters' Squadron was formed at RAF Scampton, Lincs, on 21 March 1943, specifically to train for Operation *Chastise,* the Lancaster bomber attacks on the Rhur Mohne, Eder and Sorpe dams in Germany. Having successfully completed its mission on the night 16/17 May 1943, with the aid of Dr Barnes Wallis bouncing bomb, the squadron was retained in the WW II battle order for special duties, despite AOC-in-C Bomber Command Sir Arthur 'Bomber' Harris dislike of *elite* units.

Post-war it continued in the RAF's battle order successively operating Avro Lincoln B. 2, and EE Canberra light-bombers seeing service in Malaya on anti-terrorist duties, eventually becoming part of the V-bomber force until disbanding on 1 January, 1982. Reforming on 16 May 1983, as the RAF's second front-line Panavia Tornado squadron, exactly 40 years after the dams raid, in the overland strike attack role. In 1984, it participated in the USAF Strategic Air Command's Giant Voice Bombing and Navigation competition, and won both the Lemay and Meyer Trophies. During the Gulf War No. 617 Squadron's commanding officer led the TIALD element of the Tabuk detachment,the unit also provided crews for the Muharraq detachment. Operation Southern Watch aircraft deployed bearing three-letter codes based on those worn by the units Lancaster bombers during the dambusting era, with an 'AJ' prefix and hyphen before the single letter aircraft identification code. After the Gulf War the squadron remained in the TIALD role until assuming the anti-shipping strike role in 1993. Equipped with Tornado GR 1Bs, the squadron moved to Lossiemouth on 27 April 1994, where it replaced the withdrawn Blackburn Buccaneer maritime strike bombers of No. 208 Squadron that became a Reserve unit with BAe Hawks at RAF Valley. On 3 April 1995, No. 617 Squadron showed its overland attack capability when it deployed to the Turkish AB at Incirlik, to assume the Operation Warden tasking from Harrier GR 7s, implementing the no-fly zone over Iraq. Currently its GR 1B Tornados are being upgraded to GR 4 standard.

Aircraft Markings and Codes.

The original nineteen Avro Lancaster B. III (Special) delivered for dambusting operations were coded AJ- which was later retained on standard Lancaster replacements. An additional Flight used the letters KC- and later B 1 (Special) used to carry the 12,000-lb 'Grand Slam' bombs were coded YZ-. Post-war, Avro Lincoln bombers resorted to KC- codes, but all EE Canberras of the Binbrook Wing displayed the wings 'lightning flash' on the sides of the nose, with the No. 617 Squadron airplanes identified by the dark blue colour edged in gold. Avro Vulcan B 1s carried only a small squadron badge on the fuselage sides beneath the pilots cockpit. On the V-force anti-flash white painted B. 2s, three pink 'lightning flashes' were carried on the fin, but when the V-force changed to the low-level strike role the bombers were camouflaged and for a while no squadron markings were carried. Later a few planes had 'Dayglo' red 'lightning flashes' cut from plastic sheet affixed, but these was were not weather-resistant and were replaced in 1972 by a white diamond with a pale blue outline, red flashes, and yellow 'dam walls' - a representation of the squadron badge.

On Tornados the red 'lightning flash' on top of the fine was restored in the form of a red flash on a black background and a 'fighter type' rectangle with red flashes on a black background each side of the fuselage roundel below the pilot's cockpit. Individual aircraft codes on the fin were in black, edged in red, changed in 1983, from numbers to letters. The codes letters are those used by the original dambusters airplanes.

This sidewinder equipped No. 617 Squadron Tornado GR 1B clearly depicts the unit's famous
'lightning' flash on the top of the fin and on the forward fuselage each side of the national roundel

22.

Offensive Support

While Panavia Tornados carry out the long-range interdictor strike missions in all weathers, day or night, the Harrier GR 7s and Sepecat Jaguars provide the RAF with the ability to deploy air power quickly and effectively for out-of-theatre operations as in Bosnia, and Kosovo, to attack targets at shorter range. The first-generation Harriers were assigned primarily to two major roles: Close Air Support (CAS) - attacking enemy forces in contact with, or in close proximity to friendly forces - and Battlefield Air Interdiction (BAI) against enemy forces immediately behind the Forward Edge of the Battle Area (FEBA), but not yet in contact. The BAI role was especially aimed at cutting off enemy forces from their reinforcements. The CAS and BAI missions are collectively known as Offensive Support Operations (OSO).

Currently although still nominally assigned to OSO, both Harrier II GR 7s and Sepecat Jaguar GR 3 airplanes are today assigned to the short-range interdiction role, attacking enemy forces before they can be brought to bear against friendly forces, beyond the range of friendly ground-based fire support. It is the offensive support units job to attack the enemy where he is most vulnerable, forcing him to extend his air defences over a wider depth. Short-range interdiction is aimed primarily at destroying any enemy support units or 'follow-on' or reinforcements in the rear. The RAF has three front-line Harrier squadrons. Nos. 1, 3 and 4 all based at RAF Cottesmore, Rutland. All three are regularly deployed on out-of-area commitments. No. 1 Squadron has been deployed on a number of practice and front-line operations aboard Royal Navy, FAA aircraft carriers, the most important being in the South Atlantic in 1982, in the Falklands War.

The front-line Jaguar fleet consists of three squadrons: No. 6, 41, and 54 all based at RAF Coltishall, Norfolk. No. 41 Squadron is also one of the RAF's nominated tactical reconnaissance units. All three Jaguar units regularly undertake overseas deployments and at home are assigned the regional reinforcement role. In recent years both the Harrier and Jaguar have received new weapons to allow more effective medium-level operation, including the Canadian CRV-7 high-velocity rocket and the American CBU cluster bomb. Both types carry the Paveway II laser-guided bomb (LGB), with the Jaguar GR 3s able to self-designate or buddy lase using the TIALD pod. Jaguars also carry AIM 9L Sidewinder AAM on over-wing pylons,dictated by its small wing planform. The Harrier is also fully laser 'smart weapon' capable, although in the Kosovo War, it was forced to resort to WW II iron bombs which it can deliver with great accuracy, as bad weather and no radar rendered its LGBs impotent. The Harrier is to receive the new Brimstone missile for anti-armour missions and both types are expected to carry the Paveway III LGBs in the future. All single-seat Jaguars are being upgraded to GR 3A standard with improved avionics to continue in service until 2008. Forty Harrier GR 7s are to be retrofitted with 23,800-lb Mk 107 R-R Pegasus engines with deliveries between 2002 -2004. Modified aircraft are to be redesignated Harrier GR 9.

No. 6 Squadron

RAF Coltishall, Norfolk. Offensive Support, night FGA
Jaguar GR 3/GR 3A (11) T.2A/T.4 (1)
Motto :   *Oculi exercitus* - 'The eyes of the Army'
Nickname :   'Flying Tin Openers'

No. 6 Squadron is unique in that it is the RAF's longest serving unit having never been disbanded since it formed at South Farnborough, on 31 January 1914. Serving overseas for much of its existence in WW II the squadron was equipped with the 40 mm anti-tank cannon-equipped Hawker Hurricane IID variant, and participated in many of the famous campaigns in the Western Desert. This gave rise to the famous "Flying Can-openers" nickname and insignia. A short time was spent in Yugoslavia during 1945, and post-war the squadron relocated to the Near East from where it operated the D. H. Vampire, Venom and EE Canberra. Upon return to the UK No. 6 Squadron received the MDC Phantom FGR 2 and retained these until re-equipped with the Anglo-French Sepecat Jaguar at RAF Lossiemouth, Scotland, on 2 October, 1974. Moving to RAF Coltishall, Norfolk, on 6 November that year. It formed part of No. 38 Group Strike Command, whose role was to provide forces for rapid deployment and intervention overseas as and when required. Also until 1983, No. 6 Squadron was assigned to NATO's Strategic Reserve, when it became a Regional Reinforcement squadron. It also fulfilled commitments to NATO's ACE Mobile Force and to the UKMF. The squadron saw distinguished service in the Gulf War and since has borne its share of the rotational deployments to Incirlik, Turkey, for participation in Operation *Warden,* and to Italy for Operation *Deny Flight* over the Balkans and later in the Kosovo War in April 1999. No. 6 Squadron pilot's were the first to fly operational TIALD sorties over Bosnia, and designated targets for the LGB-equipped Harriers during Operation *Deliberate Force* in the region in November 1995.

No. 6 Squadron Sepecat
Jaguar T.2A

Aircraft Markings and Codes

Official markings were first carried on No. 6 Squadrons B.E. 2c airplanes in 1916. Three fuselage bands, one each side of the roundel and one just forward of the tailplane. The bands were black on clear doped airplanes and white on khaki drab planes. Similar markings were used on R.E. 8s until March 1918, when all marking was removed. Bristol Fighters carried a white "6" on the fin superimposed on a pointed star. This was later changed to an eagle preying on a serpent shaped like a six. Later this unofficial badge appeared with a red shield as background, later augmented with a gunners stripe painted diagonally across the fin.

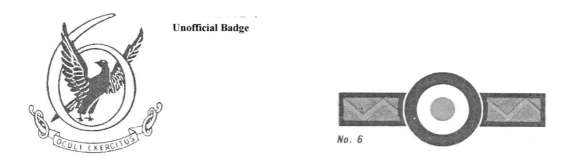

Unofficial Badge

OCULI EXERCITUS

No. 6

Fairey Gordons were similarly marked with the flight commanders and C. O.'s aircraft having individual coloured fins. More restrained markings were used on Hawker Harts, Demons and Hardys. Harts carried only a unit badge and shield on the fin. Demons and Hardys had no unit markings until after the Munich Crisis when ZD- codes appeared. In April, 1939, XE- codes were allocated but never carried. JV- was introduced at the outbreak of WW II and carried on various airplanes types intermittently until 1943, when only individual codes were used. With the arrival of Hawker Hurricane IVs the JV- code re-appeared and was subsequently carried by Supermarine Spitfires and Hawker Tempest with the gunners stripe flanking the squadron badge on the fin from 1949 onwards.

D. H. Vampires had the insignia moved to the sides of the nose and individual airplane letters were painted on the twin booms at the rear below the tail 'acorn'. A small "flying tin-opener" motif was painted on the rudders. The camouflaged D. H. Venoms had the gunners stripe re-instated as rectangular-shaped light-blue markings with a red zig-zag stripe on each side of the fuselage markings also a squadron badge on the nose and from 1957, the "Flying Tin-Opener" motif appeared on the tip-tanks in red.

EE Canberras kept the "tin-opener" emblem with gunners stripe on the fin. When the MDC Phantom II was introduced the "Tin-Opener" emblem was superimposed on a white disc painted on the fin along with the last three figures of the airplanes official registration (i.e XV 480) although by 1971, the gunners stripe re-appeared on the fin and the emblem on the nose. On the introduction of low-viz camouflage, national markings and serials were toned down.

Sepecat Jaguars carried similar markings until 1981, when the two-letter identification codes were introduced the suffix "E" donating "Six" squadron. Currently the gunners stripe is carried on the RWR aerial casing, with the "Flying Tin-Opener" motif on the engine intakes.

No. 16(R) Squadron

RAF Coltishall, Norfolk. Jaguar aircrew conversion.
Jaguar GR 3/GR 3A/T.2A/T.4 (8)
Motto : *Operta aperta* 'Hidden things are revealed'
Nickname : "Saints"

No. 16 Squadron was formed at St Omer, France, in February 1915 as a Corp reconnaissance unit to serve on the Western Front. Between the wars the squadron continued in the army support or ground-attack role. Initially on return from France operating from Salisbury Plain, in Wiltshire in support of the army, with A. W. Atlas, Audax, and Hawker Hector biplane bombers, before going to France with its Westland Lysander in 1939. Later a change of role saw the squadron undertake tactical reconnaissance duties with north American Mustang, Tomahawk and successive marks of Spitfires from the Mk XI onwards from September 1943 until March 1946. The squadron was then assigned to RAF Germany as a ground-attack unit with Hawker Tempest FB.5 and F.2 fighter planes, D. H. Vampire FB.5 and D. H. Venom FB.1

From 1958, the squadron was RAF Germany's senior strike unit equipped EE Canberra B(I) Mk 8 interdictor strike planes, then, from January 1973, with Blackburn Buccaneer S.2B strike bombers. Panavia Tornado strike planes were received on 29 February 1984, along with a full complement of fully worked-up crews at RAF Laarbruch, to form the 'Laarbruch Wing' alongside Nos. 2, XV, and 20 Squadrons. The unit finally disbanded in Germany on 11 September 1991 until April 1992, when the Jaguar OCU, No. 226 took over the No. 16 (Reserve) Squadron number-plate.

No. 226OCU

GR 3B has a day out at the airshow, parked displaying it's red/white fuselage blanking protection ribbons

Aircraft markings and codes.

The unofficial 'Saint' emblem carried by No. 16 Squadron dates back to St Omer, France, in WW I when the unit flew a miscellany of type until standardising on Royal Aircraft Factory B.E.2 in 1915. No markings were carried on the squadron's airplanes until April 1916, when a vertical bar forward and a band to the rear of the roundel was displayed, black on clear doped airplanes and white on khaki drab planes. The same markings were used on later model B. E. 2s and R. E. 8s until March 1918, when all unit markings was removed from Corp reconnaissance airplanes. Army co-operation F 2bs were also believed to be devoid of markings, but the A.W. Atlas had a single band painted aft of the roundel. Similar markings were used on the Hawker Audax but moved forward of the roundel. From 1937, the 'cross keys' centre piece of the squadron's badge was painted on the Audaxes fin within a six -pointed star. After the Munich Crisis of 1938, Westland Lysander army co-operation airplanes were annotated official KJ- codes, changed to EE- in April 1939, and then UG- before the squadron left for France with the BEF, the code remaining until Lysanders were withdrawn in 1942. Although some of the squadron's North American Mustang I fighters may have also carried UG-identification, but on joining the 2nd TAF in Germany no unit markings were carried until the squadron re-equipped with Hawker Tempest F.2 fighters in April, 1947. The Tempest and D.H Vampire FB.5 that followed carried the official code EG-.

The pre-war black band now edged in yellow was re-introduced on D. H. Venom FB Is and the same marking was used on the EE Canberra B(I)8 interdictor strike planes, the band displayed either side of the fuselage roundel. For a time the Canberras wore the rather gaudy sharkmouth 'jaws', commonplace on American fighter and ground attack planes in WW II. Large airplane serials were painted in white on the rear fuselage and the black and yellow 'cross keys' insignia on a yellow-edged white disc appeared on the sides of the nose beneath the cockpit. With the arrival of Blackburn Buccaneer strike planes markings became more subdued. The nose insignia was removed and the serials painted in black, but the now famous black band was retained and the unofficial 'Saint' marking that appeared in the early 1970s on Canberras on the fin, was retained on Buccaneers on the fin just below the bullet fairing. The black band now became a black arrowhead edged in yellow painted on the nose ahead of the roundel, with the 'cross keys' insignia displayed on the sides of the engine air intakes. Panavia Tornados retained the same combination of markings except the arrowhead was superseded by yellow edged black bars flanking the roundel on the nose below the pilot's cockpit. While black and gold 'cross keys' appeared on the sides of the large rectangular air intakes, and the "Saint" high on the tail appeared on a black disc centred on a yellow-edged black stripe on the RWR fairing. The unit codes letter 'F' together with the airplanes identification letter was also on the fin in black edged in yellow. Aircraft codes FA to FZ being used.

No. 16

Jaguar strike plane in winter camouflage

27.

No. 41 (F) Squadron

RAF Coltishall, Norfolk. Offensive Support/Tactical Recce
Jaguar GR 3/GR 3A (12) T.4 (1)
Motto : Seek and destroy

No. 41

No. 41 Squadron formed on 14 July 1916, receiving F. E. 8s for scouting and remained in this role throughout and between the wars. Reforming in 1929, the squadron successively operated Sopwith Snipes, A. W. Siskin, Bristol Bulldog, Hawker Demon and Fury fighters before receiving Supermarine Spitfires just before the start of WW II. The squadron flew the Spitfire throughout the Battle of Britain, over France and against the V1s until it re-equipped with Hawker Tempest when it became part of the forces of occupation in Germany. It disbanded on 1 April 1946, being renumbered No. 26 Squadron. Reformed the same day assuming No. 122 Squadron number-plate it flew Spitfires again by way of the Mk 21, receiving D. H. Hornet twin-engined fighters in 1948, and later Meteors and Hunters. Gloster Javelin all-weather night fighters were received in January 1958and after five years (Sept 65 - Sept 70) as a Bloodhound II SAM unit at RAF West Raynham, it reformed as a front-line flying unit in April 1972, with MDC Phantom FGR 2 at Coltishall. Having converted to the Sepecat Jaguar in August 1976, along with its co-located cousins it served with distinction in the Gulf War and since that period played its part in support of Operation *Warden* in Turkey. It also trains up some of the ground attack 'jocks' to fly reconnaissance sorties to help 'spread the load' on operational detachments.

No. 41 Squadron Jaguar GR 1B with tactical recce-pod fitted

Aircraft Markings and Codes

No. 41 Squadron's F. E. 8 carried no unit markings, but at one stage did feature large identification numerals on each side of the gunner's cupola and across the centre section of the upper mainplane. Airco D. H. 5 airplanes had a vertical white bar painted each side of the roundel, and this marking was also used on S.E. 5A fighters until March 1918, when it changed to two bars aft of the roundel. Following reformation in 1923, the squadron's airplanes started to carry a red stripe along the sides of the fuselage and across the span of the upper mainplane between the roundels. Versions of this basic unit marking appeared on a succession of type with Hawker Demons also carrying the Cross of Lorraine on the fin. Camouflaged Supermarine Spitfires introduced the official code letters PN- allocated after the Munich Crisis of 1938. Later, the code changed to EB- in September 1939, and this appeared on all Spitfire variants operated by the squadron throughout the war.

In 1947, an attempt was made to re-introduce the pre-war red stripe, but this was not greeted with much enthusiasm by those in authority and the official EB- code continued to be carried until early 1951. During 1950, however a miniature version of of the red stripe on either side of a white diamond enclosing the double-armed cross emblem had appeared on the fins of D. H. Hornet F. 1, F. 3, and the red stripe was painted on the Gloster Meteor day fighters in the form of bars either side of the roundel. To make them more prominent, thin white stripes were added to the top and bottom of the bars, and these were enhanced on Hawker Hunter airplanes which had the marking on either side of a white outlined red cross on the nose. The same marking was used on the squadron's Gloster Javelin all-weather fighters on the tail-fins. The MDC Phantoms had the same markings on the nose and the Sepecat Jaguars also carried the Cross of Lorraine on the fin, outlined in white and surmounted by a gold crown and the Roman numerals 'XLI'.

No. 41 Squadron spent five years as a Bloodhound SAM unit in the East of England from September 1965 to September 1970. It is of interest, throughout their service life, in great secrecy, Bloodhound SAMs were serviced at RAF Church Fenton, Yorkshire. The station at the time being officially home to No 7 Flying Training School.

No. 41 Squadron GR 3 armed for patrol over Iraq Operation Warden. Fitted AIM 9L Sidewinder, Phimat ALQ-101 and two 454 kg bombs

The 'Old' Sepecat GR 1 Jaguar office

The 'New' upgraded GR 3 Sepecat office

Photograph British Aerospace

No. 54 Squadron

RAF Coltishall, Norfolk. Offensive Support,
Jaguar GR 3/GR 3A (11) T.2A/T.4 (1)
Motto : *Audax omnia perpeti* 'Boldness to endure anything'

No. 54

'Always-a-fighter unit', No. 54 Squadron formed on 15 May 1916, at Castle Bromwich, as a scout unit, the first to proceed to France with Sopwith Pups. Disbanding a year after the Armistice at Yatesbury, Wilts, it reformed in 1930 with A. W. Siskin, followed by Bristol Bulldogs and then Gloster Guantlet and Gloster Gladiator before receiving the new Supermarine Spitfire monoplane fighters just before the war. After operating with distinction in the Battle of Britain and the following offensive operations over France, the squadron was posted to Australia where it operated in defence of Darwin in the Northern Territory and subsequently in the Pacific area.

Returning to the UK in October 1945, it rejoined Fighter Command to operate Hawker Tempest, and then D. H. Vampire jets followed by Gloster Meteor and Hawker Hunter day fighters. Superseded by MDC Phantoms and Sepecat Jaguar GR 1s on 29 March 1974 at RAF Lossiemouth, Scotland, as the RAF's first front-line Jaguar squadron. The unit moving to Coltishall four months later on 15 August 1974. The squadron was assigned to the Offensive Support role and formed part of SACUER's Strategic Reserve until the 1 January 1983, after which it was re-designated as a NATO Regional Reinforcement squadron with a designated base at Tirstrup in Denmark. During one of the rotational deployments to the Italian air base at Gioia del Colle, as part of operation *Deny Flight* in the mid-90s the squadron's pilots took part in the NATO strike against Udbina airfield.

Aircraft Markings and Codes

Soon after No. 54 Squadron's arrival on the Western Front approval was given for the unit to carry official markings, and the squadron's Sopwith Pups were soon carrying a white horizontal bar along the upper longeron of the fuselage forward of the tailplane. On Sopwith Camels this was changed to a white band forward of the roundels, and in March 1918, the marking became a white zig-zag painted between the roundel and the tailplane.

When the squadron reformed in 1930, with A. W. Siskin the squadron marking was a yellow stripe painted across the upper mainplane between the roundels and along the rear fuselage sides. Later the squadron requested, and received, permission to change the markings to a red band with oblique white bars across it, and this was introduced on Gloster Gauntlets from September, 1936. However, with the introduction of Gladiators the airplanes fins were coloured to denote the Flight and status of the pilot, and also carried a white 'spearhead'

No 54 Squadron Sepecat Jaguar accentuating the units yellow and blue chequers   *Photograph British Aerospace, Kingston*

As with other front-line units the Munich Crisis of 1938,brought an official unit code DL-, which was probably not used until Supermarine Spitfire Is were received in March, 1939. In September 1939, the code changed to KL- and this was used until the squadron left for Australia in June 1942. In Australia, No. 54 Squadron reverted to its pre-wartime code DL-, which was usually painted in white forward of SEAC-type roundels.

On return to the UK, No. 54 Squadron adopted the official HF- code formerly allotted to No. 183 Squadron, and used it on Hawker Tempest II and D. H. Vampire F. I jets but not on the F. 3s which were unmarked apart from a squadron badge carried on the nose until 1948, when blue and yellow checks were added as flanking bars. Some airplanes also had blue tailplanes with a yellow stripe across them. Gloster Meteor F. 8s had enlarged checks positioned on each side of the fuselage roundel, but Hawker Hunter day fighters saw the the markings restored to the nose of the airplane flanking the unit badge, and an individual letter on the fin. Similar markings were applied to the squadrons MDC Phantoms, but on Sepecat Jaguars the checks were moved to the engine intakes and the lion badge on the nose was painted blue on a yellow shield. In 1981, the suffix 'G' was added to the airplanes identification letter, to indicate the squadron.

XZ367(GP) of No 54 Squadron and XZ363(FO) formate over the arrid terrain of Eastern Turkey   (RAF)

The strike planes are en-route to police the 'No-fly' zone. Note all unit markings are removed

No. 54 Squadron airplanes
Camouflage & European low-viz

33.

Air Defence

Responsibility for the air defence of the United Kingdom is the premise of the Panavia Tornado F. 3 Air Defence Variant. Successive defence cuts and the lease of twenty-four airplanes to Italy have seen the number of RAF interceptor squadrons drastically reduced, the most recent unit to disband being No. 5 Squadron in early 2002. Nevertheless those that remain will continue to play a vital role for many years until the Eurofighter becomes fully operational towards the end of the decade.

Introduction of the Air Defence Variant (ADV) of the Panavia Tornado with its powerful GEC/ Ferranti A.I. 24 Foxhunter radar in a lengthened radome marked more than just a change of type in the air intercept inventory, since it was just one element of a radical overhaul of the entire British air defence system. It was, but one part of a new air defence infrastructure, known as — the Integrated UK Air Defence Ground Environment (UKADGE), with new control centres and reporting stations and a network of mobile air defence radars. The new system became operational in 1992-93 and was formally commissioned on 1 June, 1993.

No. 229 OCU at RAF Coningsby, began training instructors for the ADV force in 1985, using 18 F.2 variants referred to as 'Blue Circle Radar' airplanes. Minus their Foxhunter radars, due to late delivery by the manufacturer GEC/Marconi, this was in fact a misnomer, as indeed to maintain the airplanes centre-of-gravity (CoG) steel bars were fitted in the nose equivalent to the weight of the A.I. 24 radar. The first flight of a Tornado fitted with A.I.24, took place on 17 June, 1981 nearly a year behind schedule although at one time the project was running nearly three years late ! Nevertheless the first Tornado ADV squadron began conversion at the end of 1986, followed by one every six months until the last became operational in 1990 at RAF Leeming, Yorkshire.

The RAF formed seven front-line Tornado F. 3 squadrons and the OCU once it received its own F. 3s also had a front-line commitment by way of Reserve squadron status. Five squadrons were controlled originally by SACUER (Supreme Allied Commander Europe) through No 11 Group, Strike Command, and they were responsible for defence of the UK Air Defence Region which formed the bulk of the NATO AEW Area 12. The remaining two squadrons were declared to SACLANT (Supreme Allied Commander Atlantic) for maritime air defence duties, though they also took their turn in providing airplanes for QRA (Quick Reaction Alert), whereby at least two airplanes are maintained ready for immediate 'scramble' twenty-fours a day, seven days a week, all year round, should there be any unidentified intrusion into the UK's airspace.

The operational F.3 units were based initially at RAF Coningsby, Lincs, and RAF Leuchars in Scotland, existing fighter bases with HAS (Hardened Aircraft Shelters), both having formerly operated the MDC F-4 Phantom IIs. Later RAF Leeming, Yorks, a former Flying Training Command base was also given over to ADV Tornado operations as well as radar air intercept training with the arrival of a squadron of BAe Hawks as well as training of FACs (Forward Air Controllers), using the same airplanes. The Northern QRA commitment was shared between the squadron's at Leeming and Leuchars, while the Coningsby based units along with No. 74 "Tiger" Squadron at RAF Wattisham, Suffolk, equipped with former US Navy Phantom IIs were responsible for the Southern QRA area.

However, the end of the Cold War meant a dramatic reduction in 'trade' for the ADV Tornados with incursions into UK airspace by Soviet MiG-25 'Foxbat' high-speed reconnaissance planes and Tupolev 'Bear' long-range strategic bombers virtually a thing of the past. Gradually the QRA commitment was scaled down, and from the 9 January 1992, was maintained only at RAF Leuchars, with crews drawn from the other stations sharing the burden if necessary. At the same time a VC 10 in-flight refuelling tanker was maintained on alert at RAF Brize Norton, Oxon, ready to scramble in support if necessary.

Front and Rear Cockpits F.3 Tornado
Note: Outmoded black and white TV
Tabulator Displays, to be replaced by full
colour MFDs in the airplanes F.3 2000
upgrade programme

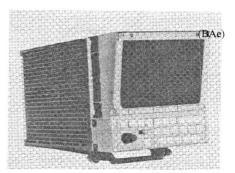

(BAe)

The TV tabular display for the Panavia Tornado

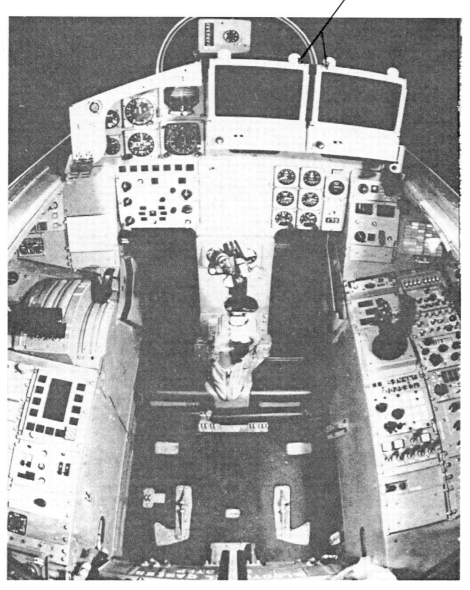

35.

Tornado Nose Radars

The GR. 1's front end actually houses two radars and associated LRUs (Line Replaceable Units)
The Texas Instruments pulse-doppler multi-mode radar with ground mapping and its terrain-following sub-unit

The Panavia Tornado F.3 ADV's front end is taken up with the powerful A.I 24 Foxhunter radar

Almost all of the powerful GEC/Marconi A.I.24 Foxhunter radars are now to Stage 2 Plus standard

The Ferranti LRMTS—Lasar Ranger and Marked Target Seeker—used in the RAF's BAe Harriers and Sepecat Jaguar airplanes

Soviet Mikoyan MiG-25 'Foxbat' Mach 3.0 (2.8) High altitude, High Speed Reconnaissance Plane

38.

Soviet Tupolev Tu-142 'Bear'

39.

Although RAF ADV Tornados played a prominent role in the Gulf War, flying CAP (Combat Air Patrol) and indeed were the first on the scene when Saddam Hussein's forces invaded Kuwait. None were involved in any actual combat operations. Soon after the end of the Cold War the Government seized the chance to cut back on the hard pressed fighter units, with barely enough left to meet all their home-based and overseas commitments. No. 74 Squadron's F-4 Phantom IIs were the first to go, and it was decided not to upgrade the original F.2 airplanes to F. 3 standard. Luckily the airframes were stored to be used later to salvage a number of F. 3 airframes damaged by a civil contractor while undergoing modification work at the RAF St Athan maintenance depot. No. 23 Squadron disbanded on 28 February 1994, and as already mentioned 24 airplanes were long-leased to Italy, although a number have already been returned as the Italians who are not entirely happy with the F. 3s serviceability, have decided instead, to lease thirty Lockheed Martin F-16 ADF variants to fulfil its interim fighter requirement until the first Eurofighter Typhoons enter AMI (Aeronautica Militare Italiane.) service. However, the disbandments gave rise to a number of surplus airplanes and from 1993, the RAF increased the establishment of its F.3 Tornado squadron's from 15 to 18 aircraft, beginning with Nos. 43 and 111 Squadrons. Although subsequently under the Strategic Defence Review requirements and overseas commitments this has dropped back to a nominal 13 airplanes.

Under Operation *Grapple* Tornado F. 3 units maintained a detachment at the Italian, Gioia del Colle AB for operations over Bosnia, policing the 'No-Fly' Zone imposed by the United Nations until mid-1996. While, since 1992, four ADV Tornados have been deployed in the South Atlantic with No. 1435 Flight to provide air defence for the Falkland Islands and maintain the 250 miles air exclusion zone against incursion's by Argentine aircraft on occasions.

AMI 36 Stormo Panavia Tornado F.3 ADV variant on lease (Photo T. Shia)

No. 11 Squadron

RAF Leeming, Yorks. Air Defence/CAP.
Panavia Tornado F. 3 (12)
Motto : *Ociores acrioresqe aquillis*
'Swifter and keener than eagles'

No. 11 Squadron formed at Netheravon on 14 February 1915, the first dedicated RFC fighter unit in WW I successively operating a variety of types including the Vickers Gunbus, FE 2b and Bristol Fighter. Following the Armistice it served in India, operating such types as the Westland Wapiti and Hawker Hart on policing duties in the North West Frontier. During WW II the squadron moved to the Middle East as a light-bomber unit and took part in the Greek Campaign before again departing for India and the Pacific theatre with Hawker Hurricane and Supermarine Spitfire fighters. Post-WW II the unit re-established itself in Germany in 1948, as a D. H. Mosquito-equipped strike-fighter unit. Subsequently operating D. H. Vampire, Venom and Gloster Javelin all-weather night fighters before disbanding in January 1966.

The squadron reformed in April 1967, at RAF Leuchars, Scotland, to operate the supersonic EE Lightning on Air Defence duties. Ten years later the unit stood down as a Lightning squadron and began to receive Panavia Tornado F. 3s as No 11 Squadron (Designate) at RAF Coningsby, Lincs, on 25 April 1988, officially reforming on 1 July, 1988, at RAF Leeming, Yorkshire. Unlike the other RAF Leeming squadrons, No. 11 was not based in a modern HAS complex instead operating from the base's old C-Type hangars, with a conventional 'line'. It was able to do this as it assumed the 'mobile' maritime defence role, previously undertaken by the 'Fighting Cocks', No. 43 Squadron, this role variously demanding operation from FOBs (forward operating bases).

The squadron was declared operational to SACLANT in November 1988. On 30 August 1990, No 11 Squadron provided crews for the Tornado ADV detachment (Operation *Granby*) based at Dhahran, Saudia Arabia to carry out CAP (Combat Air Patrol) over Northern Saudia Arabia. But, No 11 Squadron's crews did not take any part in the Gulf War (Desert Storm) having returned to the UK in early December 1990. Later equipped with the developed 'Stage-One Plus' A. I. 24 radars it was the first of the RAF's F. 3 Tornado squadrons to participate in operations over Bosnia, deploying to Gioia del Colle, Italy, on the night of 18/19 April, 1993. Later in 1994, following the NATO raid on Udbina on 21 November, the squadron's airplanes came under fire from the ground whilst on CAP on 24 November. Subsequent deployments to the Italian base by Tornado F.3 ADV units were for three months duration on rotation.

Aircraft Markings and Codes

No unit markings appeared on No. 11 Squadron airplanes until they received Bristol Fighters in June 1917. These airplanes had sloping white bars on the fuselage either side of the roundel. Silver painted Airco D. H. 9As, Fairey Fawns and Horsleys carried no squadron markings, although in India a broad vertical stripe was painted around the fuselage forward of the roundel, also the airplanes carried a large individual letter on the forward fuselage. Later Hawker Harts carried a representative badge on a white disc on the fin, and had two red bands around the aft fuselage with a small individual letter on the top coaming just to the rear of the gunners cockpit.

In 1938, the official code OY- was allocated but probably not carried. While in the Far East the squadrons Bristol Blenheims carried the code YH-, although when in the Western Desert and Greece AD- was used. Hawker Hurricane and Supermarine Spitfire fighters carried individual airplane letters and SEAC (South-East Asia Command) white bands across the wings, tailplanes, fins and rudders. D. H. Mosquitos were officially marked with the EX- code. This code also carried on D.H. Vampire FB 5s until the 2nd TAF adopted a single letter code "L", carried on the booms forward of the roundel with a letter of similar size aft in black; outlined in white on camouflaged airplanes.

D. H. Venoms carried similar markings with additional black rectangles with yellow triangles superimposed either side of the roundel. These markings were retained on the Meteors also the Gloster Javelin FAW 4s which also had a white disc carrying the individual airplane letter in black. On the FAW 9s the white disc was replaced by a broad black stripe with a tapering yellow flash superimposed on the fin immediately below the tailplane.

Whilst No. 11 Squadron was No. 228 OCU Shadow Squadron two buff coloured eagles with yellow beaks and talons were painted on a white disc on the fin. EE Lightning all-weather interceptors reverted to black rectangles with yellow triangles on either side of the nose roundels with an "eagle" badge on a white disc on the fin. By the mid-1970s the "eagles" had been enlarged and painted directly on the fin in dark brown, with yellow beaks and talons. With the 'toned down' markings on the squadron Mk 6 Lightnings of the mid-1980s when the airplanes received their medium sea grey with barley grey undersides, miniature black rectangles with yellow triangles either side of the "eagles" appearing on the fin. Individual airplane letters were in white, prefixed by the squadron letter "B" near the top of the fin.

Similar markings have been adopted for the ADV Tornados although the rectangular emblem has been moved to the nose either side of the pilot's cockpit. With enlarged "eagles" on the tail with the individual airplane lettering in black and the new squadron identity letter "D" preceding it in black.

No. 11 Sqandron F.3 Tornado on the flight-line

Two No. 11 Squadron F. 3s on approach, Leeming base.   (T. Shia)

This black-tailed aircraft "DH" C. O.'s Wg Cdr. David Hamilton's mount

No. 25 Squadron

RAF Leeming, Yorks. Air Defence/CAP.
Panavia Tornado F. 3 (12)
Motto : *Feriens tego* "Striking I defend"

No. 25

Formed on 26 September, 1915, No. 25 Squadron served as both a fighter and day bomber unit operating a variety of types in France during WW I. Between the wars it returned to the fighter role using Sopwith Snipes, Gloster Grebes, A. W. Siskin and Hawker Furies, to name but a few. Almost immediately before WW II the squadron converted to Bristol Blenheim specialising in night-fighting, these followed by Bristol Beaufighters in October 1940. D. H. Mosquitos were received in 1943, to be used on intruder operations and also the battle against the V 1. D. H. Vampires followed by Meteor night-fighters and Gloster Javelin all-weather fighters were used post-war until 30 November 1962, when the squadron disbanded at RAF Leuchars. A year later the squadron commenced more than two decades at home and in Germany as a SAM Bloodhound unit until returning to the all-weather fighter role in January 1990.

After twenty-six years with Bloodhound SAMs, No.25 Squadron reformed as a ADV unit with the Panavia F.3 Tornado. On 30 September 1989, the squadron passed its missiles to No.85 Squadron, as No. 25 Squadron (Designate) had formed on 1 July 1989, to be officially re-established on 1 October at RAF Leemings second HAS complex. The first Tornado F.3s were received at Leeming on 15 December 1988. With the next five airplanes delivered on 3 July 1989, No.25 Squadron was declared operational on type, on 1 January 1990. Today (2002) the unit is still operating the ADV Tornado at its north Yorkshire base.

Aircraft markings and codes
The squadron's F.E. 8s did not carry unit markings, but the D. H. 4 day bombers appeared with a white crescent immediately behind the roundel and individual identification letters to the rear. Post-WW I the squadron's silver finish Sopwith Snipes were distinguished by their coloured fins. Later on return from the Middle East and re-equipment with Gloster Grebe biplanes two parallel black stripes were painted across the top wings and also along the fuselage sides. The same markings were used on A. W. Siskins and the Hawker Fury fighters on which the fuselage stripe tapered to a point under the tailplane. Camouflaged Gloster Gladiators may have been similarly marked but the Munich Crisis brought the official RX- code. Changed in September 1939, on the units Bristol Blenheim airplanes to ZK-, the unit code carried on all the squadrons airplanes until the 1950s.

Minature parallel black stripes appeared on D. H. Mosquito NF. 36 in 1949, and this marking appeared on the D. H. Vampire FB 5s in the form of black rectangles each side of the boom roundels. On Meteor night-fighters this was changed to black-edged silver rectangles each side of the rear fuselage roundel, a similar marking used on Gloster Javelin all-weather night-fighters was moved to the top of the fin, the airplane also carrying the unit badge superimposed on the rectangle. Later this badge was more prominently displayed by splitting a smaller rectangle into two parts above a large individual identification letter, which was repeated on the sides of the nose. Bloodhound missiles carried no unit markings. Panavia Tornado F. 3 airplanes displayed the hawk on a glove from the units badge on the fin with the RWR casing outlined in black forming a rectangle, airplane identification letters in the FA to FZ range in white outlined in black.

No. 25 Squadron 75th Anniversary livery depicting the units campaign honours below the cockpit (T. Shia)

No. 25 Squadron F.3 resplendent in an 'alternative' 75th Anniversary livery (T.Shia)

No. 29(R) Squadron

RAF Coningsby, Lincs. Eurofighter OCU (2004)
Eurofighter Typhoon
Motto: *Impiger et acer* - 'Energetic and keen'

No. 29

No. 29 Squadron is another 'always a fighter' squadron since it formed on 7 November, 1915, at Gosport. Its first airplanes were Airco D. H. 2s then French Nieuports and S.E.5As in France in WW I. After the war it was disbanded for three years before re-forming at RAF Duxford, Cambs, with Sopwith Snipe in April, 1923. These were replaced by A. W. Siskin when the squadron moved to RAF North Weald, Essex, in 1928, and it subsequently received Bristol Bulldog and Hawker Demons. A. I. radar-equipped Bristol Blenheims were flown in the Battle of Britain, these being supplanted by Beaufighters in 1941. D. H. Mosquito VIIs arrived in May, 1943 and successive marks were flown until 1951, when Meteor jets were used, followed by Gloster Javelin all-weather night fighters. In 1963, the squadron went to Cyprus and then Zambia before returning to the UK to become a Wattisham-base EE Lightning squadron. On 1 January the Lightning was supplanted by the MDC Phantom FGR 2 and later in April, 1987, No. 29 Squadron became the first operational Tornado ADV F. 3 unit with a maritime defence role and other out of area commitments. Interestingly No. 29 Squadron was chosen to participate in Operation *Golden Eagle,* in which four of the squadron's airplanes circumnavigated the world. En-route they took part in Malaysian and Thai air defence exercises and in air shows in Sydney, Australia, and Harrisburg, Philadelphia, USA. The squadron's crews were involved in the initial emergency deployment to the Gulf from the APC (Armament Practice Camp) in Akrotiri, Cyprus, and the squadron also provided most of the ADV Tornado crews for the Composite squadron's who flew in the war itself, on each occasion, flying under the auspices of either Nos 5 and 43 Composite Squadrons. The squadron was granted the Battle Honour 'Gulf 1991', but without the right of emblazonment. As part of the 'New' Labour Governments Strategic Defence Review, No. 29 Squadron ceased to operate the F.3 Tornado at its Lincolnshire, base on 30 October, 1998. Its aircraft re-distributed amongst the remaining ADV units. Now in 2002, it has been earmarked to reform at RAF Coningsby with the Eurofighter as the Operational Conversion Unit to begin operations in 2004 to train pilots for the operational units to form at RAF Leeming and RAF Leuchars replacing the Tornado F.3s in 2006 and 2008 respectively.

Eurofighter Typhoon with it's formidable weapon load on display Paris Air Salon 2001

Aircraft markings and codes

The squadrons D. H. 2s were unmarked, but the silver painted Nieuports that it received in the spring of 1917, carried a red band around the fuselage immediately forward of the tailplane, and Flight colours were painted on the wheel discs. With the introduction of camouflage in December 1917, the markings changed to, a white vertical stripe painted on each side of the fuselage roundel. On the SE 5A fighter, the aft fuselage band was re-introduced, but in white, and aircraft codes were painted under the wings, on 'B' Flight airplanes or on the engine cowling on 'A' Flight airplanes.

In the inter-war period the squadron carried various combinations of 'X's along the fuselage sides, this supposedly to have originated in the mid-1920s when a member of the ground staff, on being told to paint the squadrons number on the airplanes in Roman numerals, used three 'X's. In 1936, when the squadron re-equipped with Turret Demons, the 'X's were deleted and a representation of the unit badge was displayed on the fin within a red-outlined white 'spearhead'. Following the Munich Crisis of 1938, the official code YB- was allotted to No. 29 Squadron and carried on Bristol Blenheim 1Fs until September, 1939, when it changed to RO-. After the war D. H. Mosquitos also carried the squadron badge on the fin, but with the introduction of Meteor jets the 'X' marking re-appeared, this time on a red-outline white rectangle on each side of the fuselage roundel, with individual airplane code letters painted on the fin.

Gloster Javelin all-weather fighters carried similar markings, but in a single rectangle on the fin, while EE Lightnings carried the marking on the nose again, on each side of the roundel. The individual code letter appeared in black on the fin together with a representation of the unit badge. The MDC Phantoms appeared with the now familiar 'X's across the upper fin, while the centre-piece of the badge was superimposed on a large white shield on the nose.

The introduction of low-viz marked light grey camouflage, saw the three 'X's displayed in red on a white background across the airplanes RWR casing, and on the side of the miniature roundel on the engine air intakes. Also on the fin was a 'shield' badge, and the rudder carried the airplanes individual code letter in white. The similarly marked Tornado F. 3s had three red 'X's painted diagonally on the side of the engine air intakes, while the eagles of the unit emblem, one in yellow and the other in red, were positioned on the fin above the serial together with a two-letter code in the BA to BZ sequence, also in red, displayed high up on the fin. What markings are to be displayed on the Eurofighter remains to be seen, but what can be certain is the squadrons famous three 'X's will again be prominent.

RAF ZH588 Eurofighter displaying stores   (BAe)

No. 43 Squadron

RAF Leuchars, Scotland. Air Defence/CAP.
Panavia Tornado F. 3 (13)
Motto : *Gloria finis* 'Glory in the end'
Nickname : 'Fighting Cocks'

No. 43

No. 43 Squadron is another 'always-a-fighter' squadron since forming at Stirling, Scotland, on 15 April 1916, for service in France. Operating a variety of types on the Western Front during WW I, No. 43 Squadron took its Sopwith Snipes to Germany at the end of the war, returning to disband in the UK in December, 1919. The squadron re-appeared again in 1925, at RAF Henlow, Bedfordshire, equipped with Gloster Gamecocks before moving south to RAF Tangmere, Sussex, with Hawker Fury I which were superseded by Hawker Hurricane I monoplane fighters in time for the Battle of Britain. Later the squadron was employed on night-fighter operations over France before moving to North Africa to cover the landing from Gibraltar, Operation *Torch*. Supermarine Spitfires supplanted the Hurricanes and the squadron served in Italy and southern France during the invasion before being disbanded in Italy during 1947. Reformed in 1949, at RAF Tangmere with Gloster Meteors day fighters, in August, 1954 it became the first Hawker Hunter squadron and moved to Cyprus and then to Aden in 1963, where it disbanded on 14 October 1967, with the RAF's withdrawal from the Middle East. Reformed again on 1 September 1969, at RAF Leuchars, No. 43 Squadron was one of only two RAF units to operate the MDC Phantom FG.1 Air Defence fighter variant.

During the Cold War, Leuchars was the RAF's most important fighter base, closest to the threat posed by Soviet reconnaissance planes and bombers flying down from the North Cape and through the GIUK (Greenland-Iceland-UK) gap. The units based at Leuchars performed the majority of live intercepts of Soviet intruders, with the Phantom FG.1 optimised for the task and the requirements of the Northern QRA.

However, introduction of the Panavia Tornado F. 3 with its powerful A. I. 24 Foxhunter radar to replace the ageing Phantoms saw the Leuchars base hand over the Northern QRA commitment to RAF Leeming, in Yorkshire, during 1990, by which time conversion to the ADV Tornado was well underway. No. 43 Squadron down-declared with the MDC F-4 Phantom on 30 June 1989, and reformed as a ADV Tornado unit on 23 September 1989. On 1 July 1990 the "Fighting Cocks" were declared operational but the squadron did not immediately return to its pre-Tornado routine, and the Leuchars base did not resume responsibility for Northern QRA until January 1991, due in the main to the call on the squadrons crews for duty in the Gulf War as part of the ADV Composite Squadron in theatre.

In May 1994, No. 43 Squadron deployed to Gioia del Colle, Italy, for participation in Operation *Deny Flight*. Almost ten years years later No.43 Squadron is still based at RAF Leuchars, and looks forward to at least another decade on type pending its Tornado 2000 upgrade, with colour MFDs (Multi-Functional Displays) for the Foxhunter A.I.24 radar in place of the black and white TV tabulators, 1553 databus,and AMRAAM and ASRAAM missile fits, in place of the Sidewinders and Sky Flash missiles in current use.

Aircraft Markings and Codes

In the First World War No. 43 Squadron was assigned a white triangle, painted on the fuselage sides aft of the roundel on Sopwith 1½ Strutters and Camels until March, 1918, when it was replaced by two sloping white bars, one each side of the roundel. After the war no markings were carried until black and white checks were introduced on Gloster Gamecock fighters in 1926. The chequers were painted across the span of the upper wing and on the fuselage sides. The same marking was used on all subsequent airplanes until the Munich Crisis of 1938, when camouflaged Hawker Hurricanes were allocated the NQ- code until September 1939, when it changed to FT- which was used throughout the war often with an individual airplane identification letter.

Post-war miniature black and white checks were painted across the fins of the units Supermarine Spitfires, but when Gloster Meteor jets arrived in February 1949, the official code SW- was used. In 1951, official code letters were dispensed with and the units famous checks re-appeared on the fuselage each side of the roundel of the upgraded Gloster Meteor F. 8s and on the swept-wing Hawker Hunter that followed. On Hunter F. 4s a representation of a 'fighting cock', complete with boxing gloves, appeared, but when the checks were moved to the nose of the airplane, the cockerel symbol became the same as the authorised squadron badge and was superimposed on a white disc. When the airplanes were pooled at the Khormaksar base to form the 'Aden Strike Wing', No. 43 Squadron's checks were painted on one side of the roundel and No. 8 Squadron's markings on the other — the cockerel was deleted. On reforming with F-4 Phantoms, the squadron painted the checks on the sides of the engine air intakes on each side of the roundel, but it was a further two years before the 'fighting cock' re-appeared, this time on the fin. With the introduction of light grey low-viz marking in the 1980s, the markings were toned down, the checks being miniaturised applied to the top of the fin RWR casing, the cockerel lost its white background but remained on the fin along with the airplanes individual letter ident. In 1987, two-letter codes were introduced with the suffix "A" added to permit easier identification from the other F-4 Phantom operators based at Leuchars. Panavia Tornado ADV airplanes also carry two-letter codes in white on the fin as well as a large brightly coloured cockerel. The famous chequers are again placed each side of the low-viz roundel below the pilots cockpit.

No. 43 Squadron Panavia F-3 Tornado with re-heat

49.

No. 56(R) Squadron

RAF Coningsby, Lincs   No. 229 F. 3 Tornado OCU
Panavia Tornado F. 3 (19)
Motto : *Quid si coelum ruat* 'What if Heaven falls'
Nickname : 'Firebirds'

No. 56

Formed on 9 June 1916, No. 56 Squadron built its reputation on the Western Front in WW I flying the superb S.E. 5a fighter. Reformed in the UK in 1922, at North Weald, Essex, it successively used Sopwith Snipes, Fairey Gordons, A. W. Siskins, Bristol Bulldogs, Gloster Gauntlets, and Gloster Gladiator biplanes before equipping with Hawker Hurricanes in May 1938. These were used in the Battle of Britain until the squadron was the first to receive the Hawker Typhoon in September 1941. Supermarine Spitfires were received in 1944, and later the Hawker Tempest which were retained in Germany until 1946. Reformed on Gloster Meteor F. 3 day fighters in 1946, No. 56 Squadron was the only unit to receive the disappointing Supermarine Swift fighter soon withdrawn in favour of the Hawker Hunter in May 1955. EE Lightnings were received in December 1960 at RAF Wattisham, Suffolk, with which the squadron re-located to Cyprus in 1967. On returning to Wattisham in 1975, MDC Phantom FGR.2s were received, the squadron being the last RAF unit to receive the type, which it operated until standing down with its withdrawal on 1 June 1992. The squadron being one of the last RAF units to operate the type, celebrating its withdrawal when it flew a "diamond nine" over central London in June as part of the Queens birthday flypast.

Re-equipment with the Panavia Tornado F 3 commenced on 1 July 1992, when No 229 OCU at RAF Coningsby which was previously No.65 (Reserve) Squadron, was re-titled the (Tornado) F3 OCU No.56 (Reserve) Squadron. The F.3 Tornado remains the "Firebirds" mount until this day, the conversion unit incorporated into the RAFs front-line battle order with Reserve squadron status.

Aircraft markings and codes

Soon after arriving in France in April 1917, the squadron was allocated a dumb-bell unit marking, but this was used only briefly, for in June 1917, a letter/numeral code was issued and by the end of the year an 18-in wide band was being carried around the rear fuselage of the squadrons airplanes. In March 1918, the marking changed to two thin white bars sloping inwards towards the top in the same position on the fuselage, with the individual airplane letter identification displayed immediately to the rear of the roundel. Later in Egypt, Sopwith Snipes carried a thin white band around the fuselage just to the rear of the roundel, but when the unit reformed in the UK the following year more colourful markings were adopted, with the squadron using a distinct red and white chequerboard on the fuselage sides, forward of the roundel and across the span of the top of the upper mainplane.

With various subtle changes these markings were used on Gloster Grebes, A. W. Siskin, Gloster Gauntlets and Gloster Gladiator biplanes. Camouflaged monoplane Hawker Hurricanes had a distinctive 'phoenix' motif superimposed on a white 'spearhead' on the fin. After the Munich Crisis, the official code LR- was issued to the squadron. This changed to US- in September 1939, and was used on Hawker Hurricanes, Hawker Typhoons, Supermarine Spitfires, and Hawker Tempest until disbandment on 31 March, 1946. On reforming the very next day by re-numbering No. 124 Squadron, for a while that units official ON- code was retained, but in 1947, the squadron reverted to its own US- code and to the pre-war red and white checks in 1950. The checks were carried in the form of bars each side of the fuselage roundel on the Gloster Meteor and Supermarine Swift day fighters, but on the swept-wing Hawker Hunters it appeared on the nose flanking the unit badge. Some Hunter aircraft also had chequerboard wing-tips.

Early EE Lightnings carried the chequers on the nose each side of the roundel, with the 'phoenix' moved to the fin, but when the unit became Fighter Command's official 'Firebirds' formation aerobatic team in 1963, the airplanes were painted in a more distinctive livery. This was toned down on the Lightning F. 3 variant, which had a chequerboard fin and rudder, a red fuselage spine and a large red and white arrowhead on the nose until standard 'fighter type' markings were ordered by those in high places, in 1966. Lightning F. 6 variants were then similarly marked, but carried an enlarged red and yellow 'phoenix' on the fin. MDC Phantoms retained the same scheme until European theatre low-viz grey camouflage was introduced. At the same time the nose markings were miniaturized, and the 'phoenix' was moved from the tail and superimposed on the nose chequers. Additional red and white checks were applied to the top section of the fin and rudder. All, as with all other front-line units to be removed in times of hostilities and overseas operational deployments, as in the Gulf War for example.

Currently the squadrons Panavia Tornado ADV airplanes carry the famous chequers each side of the low-viz roundel on the nose below the cockpit and the 'phoenix' on the tail-fin. Large individual airplane identification letters are carried in white on the upper portion of the fin.

(RAF)

No. 56 Squadron 'Firebirds' EE Lightning F.3 display team, from an era when it was commonplace for front-line units to provide the RAF with its aerobatic display teams.

No. 56 Squadron "Firebird" complete with compliment of semi-recessed Skyflash radar-guided missiles and AIM-9L. Sidewiders

No. 111 Squadron

RAF Leuchars, Scotland. Air Defence/CAP.
Panavia Tornado F. 3 (12)
Motto : *Adstantes* — 'Standing by (them)'
Nickname : 'Treble One'

No. 111

One of the RAF's most famous fighter squadron's is "Treble One", which was originally formed in Palestine on 1 August, 1917. It operated a miscellany of types against the Turks and as a fighter unit in Syria and Egypt before being re-designated as No.14 Squadron in February 1920. Reformed in 1923, at RAF Duxford, Cambs, with Gloster Grebes, it also successively operated Snipes, A. W. Siskin, Bristol Bulldogs and Gloster Gauntlets before becoming the first RAF Hawker Hurricane squadron in January, 1938. After operating with distinction in the Battle of Britain the squadron received its first Supermarine Spitfire in the spring of 1941, which it later took to the Mediterranean to fly from bases in North Africa, Sicily and Italy before disbanding in Austria in May, 1947. Reformed at RAF North Weald, Essex, in December 1953, with Gloster Meteor F.8 day fighters it soon replaced these with swept-wing Hawker Hunters which as the RAF's premier aerobatic team through 1957-1960 it gained world-wide acclaim for its superb displays as well as its twenty-two airplane routine performed at the 1959, Farnborough SBAC show.

Re-equipped with the EE Lightning in April 1961, the squadron operated from RAF Wattisham, Suffolk, until converting to MDC FGR 2 Phantoms at Coningsby, in the summer of 1974, being the only other operator of the FG.1 variant from June 1978. The squadron converted to Panavia Tornado F. 3 in late 1989, the second Leuchars-based squadron to do so but at the same time the last squadron in the RAF battle order to convert to the type. The squadron flew its final operational Phantom FG. 1 sortie on 31 October, 1989, four months after its co-located cousin No. 43 Squadron, had relinquished some of its Phantoms to "Treble One". After this as already stated the Northern ORA commitment passed to the RAF Leeming ADV Wing for several months. It is of interest having received F. 3 Tornados, the unit continued to fly training missions with its FG. 1 Phantoms and those obtained from No. 43 Squadron until the end of January, 1990, when a new No. 111 Squadron began to form flying its first operational sorties in May 1990, after officially reforming on the 1st of the month. The squadron declared fully operational on 1 January the following year.

More than a decade later, still fully operational with its F 3 Tornados, "Treble One" is still primarily deployed on the Air Defence of the UK from its Scottish base. The current planned mid-life (Tornado 2000) upgrades to the aircraft and its A.I.24 Foxhunter radar will secure the squadron's famous "lightning flash" a place in the RAFs battle order for many years to come. In 1999/2000 No.111 Squadron based six aircraft in Dhahran, Saudi Arabia, in support of Operation *Southern Watch* for monitoring of the no-fly zone in Southern Iraq.

Aircraft Markings and Codes

No official aircraft markings were carried by No. 111 Squadron airplanes during WW I, but individual aircraft were identified by fuselage paint schemes similar to those units operating on the Western Front in France. Soon after reforming in 1923, the squadron's Gloster Grebes, Snipes and A. W. Siskins biplanes started appearing with a black stripe down the fuselage sides and across the top mainplane between the roundels. Later, this was adopted as the official unit markings and applied to Bristol Bulldog and Gloster Gauntlet fighters, the latter also carrying a squadron badge on the fin.

Somewhat unusual for fighter squadrons of the era, the squadrons, WW II Hawker Hurricane monoplane fighters had the numerals '111' painted in various colours on the sides of the fuselage in addition to the unit badge on the fin. Following the Munich Crisis, the official code TM- was allocated to the squadron although by 1939, this had changed to JU- which was used on all the Spitfire variants flown throughout the war until changed to SW- on the IXC variants flown until disbandment in 1947. Reformed with Gloster Meteor F. 8 in 1953, the pre-war black marking was adopted and applied in the form of yellow-edged rectangles on each side of the fuselage roundel. The same markings were used on the Hawker Hunters that also had a yellow-edged black letter on the fin and a squadron badge on the forward fuselage beneath the pilots cockpit. On becoming the RAF's official aerobatic display team in 1957, various colour schemes were tried before the simple but highly effective all-over black gloss was settled on. Unit marking were confined to a small squadron badge on the nose flanked by miniature gold rectangles.

In 1958, the national roundels were outlined in white and a small individual aircraft letter was painted in red above the swept-back national fin 'flash' on the tail. The press immediately nicknamed the display team the 'Black Arrows', a name which became as well known as the 'Red Arrows' of today. when the squadron re-equipped with EE Lightnings, the standard rectangular-shaped markings were changed to a black 'lightning flash' on the nose, centred on the roundel, while a stylized squadron badge was displayed on the fin. In 1965, the squadron's new Lightning F.3 variants were adorned in a much more flamboyant paint scheme. The yellow-outlined black 'lightning flash' remained on the nose, but the fuselage dorsal spine and the vertical tail surfaces were all painted black, except for a yellow panel on which was superimposed a large squadron badge, yellow on a black disc. The squadrons F. 3 Tornados have a re-styled 'lightning flash' flanking the low-viz roundel on the forward fuselage underneath the cockpit with a distinctive black rectangle outlined in yellow high on the fin with the unit badge set in a back disc. Dual individual identification letter appear on the fin in white.

F3 'HK' (ZEE835) setting out on a QRA. Note the starboard main undercarriage wheel on final stowage

ADV Tornados escorts from Nos 43 and 111 Squadrons, for Soviet Ilyushin I-78 Midas in-flight refuelling tanker on approach RAF Fairford for IAT (MoD RAF)

No. 1435 Flight (F)   RAF Mount Pleasant, Falkland Islands, South Atlantic.
                                           Panavia Tornado F.3   Air Defence (4)
                                           Markings : Large red Maltese cross carried on fin.

In July 1941, in an endeavour to afford the island of Malta in the Mediterranean better air defences from Italian Air Force night bomber raids a special night fighter unit was formed at Inga airfield with Hawker Hurricanes surplus to the establishment of the day fighter squadrons. The unit was designated the Malta Night Fighter Unit (MNFU) under C. O. Squadron Leader George Powell-Sheddon, an experienced battle-tested fighter pilot, who in his period flying Hurricane night operations on Malta, set an example to his pilots with two "kills"at night. On 2 December 1941, the MNFU was redesignated No.1435 Flight which in April 1942 was disbanded.

On 23 July 1942, No.1435 Flight (Fighter) began to reform mainly with pilots transferred from a No.603 Squadron detachment at Takali, re-equipping with Supermarine Spitfire VB on 2 August 1942 for air defence duties. By January 1943, as the unit had become considerably larger than a Flight, with Air Ministry approval it was formally designated No.1435 Squadron with Spitfire VC (coded V-) for fighter-bomber duties flying sweeps over Sicily to attack the Italian Air Force bases from where the island raids continued to be launched and to clear the way for the Allied landings.

In October 1943, the squadron moved to Grottaglie, in southern Italy, where it formed part of the Balkan Air Force, flying ground attack missions over Albania and Yugoslavia, and local air defence missions. In February 1945, No.1435 Squadron moved to Brindisi, northern Italy, to keep within range of the German forces retreating from the Balkans. The unit had also maintained a detachment on the Adriatic island of Vis from September 1944 until April 1945. Having been withdrawn from operations in April 1945, the squadron disbanded at Gragnano, Italy, on 9 May 1945.

Following the recapture of the Falkland Islands, the area,s air defence needs were the premise of a detachment of BAe Harrier GR. 3s of the resurrected No 1435 Flight (F). From 17 October 1982, they were augmented by a detachment of nine MDC FGR 2 Phantoms drawn from No. 29 Squadron, the detachment subsequently becoming No. 23 Squadron on 1 April 1983. The opening of the new RAF Mount Pleasant airfield a year later saw the Phantom detachment reduced to four airplanes; with the Harrier echelon disbanded on 12 May, 1985. The remaining No. 23 Squadron detachment assuming the No. 1435 Flight (F) designation on 1 November 1988, when a new No. 23 Squadron equipped with F.3 ADV Tornados in the UK. No. 1435 Flight (F) re-equipped with the Tornado F. 3 in July 1992, with an initial complement of four airplanes departing RAF Coningsby for the South Atlantic on 6 July, 1992. The Flight has remained in situ ever since with the airplanes rotated to the UK for major servicing and overall as and when required. Any major components such as engines etc., if needed are transported south by Lockheed Hercules transports.

Aircraft markings and codes
The units airplanes bear the same names as the Gloster Gladiators flown by the unit during its WW II defence of Malta - *Faith, Hope, Charity* and *Desperation* — the names echoed in the use of the aircraft identification letters 'F', 'H', 'C' and 'D'. The airplanes carry a large red Maltese cross on the fin.

RAF Mt Pleasant, Falkland Islands

MDC F-4 Phantom and Panavia Tornado (No. 1435 Flt)

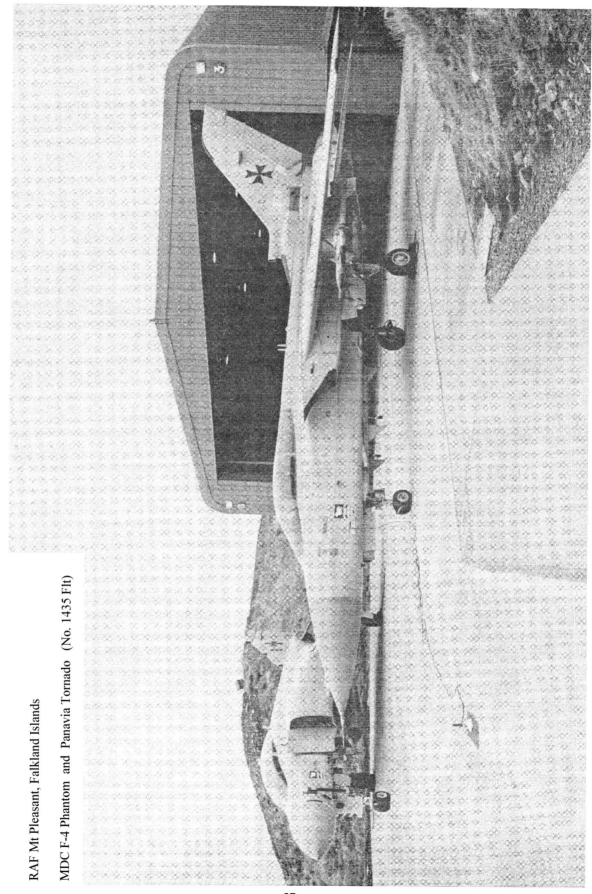

No. 100 Squadron

RAF Leeming, Yorks. Target Facilities.
BAe Hawk T.1/1A (16)
Motto : Sarang tebuan jangan dijiolok (Malay)
(Never stir up a hornet's nest)
Nickname : "Aggressors"

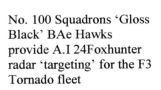

Formed in February 1917, for Home Defence, in March 1917, No. 100 Squadron moved to France as the first night-bomber unit. Subsequently operating F.E. 2, B. E. 2 and Handley Page O/400 bombers. After returning to the UK the squadron re-equipped with the Bristol Fighter and flew these in operations against the IRA during 1920/22. During the next few years it operated a miscellany of types including, Airco D. H. 9s, Vickers Vimy, Hawker Horsley and Vickers Vildebeest torpedo-bombers, the squadron moving to Singapore with the latter type in 1933. These were all lost in the Japanese attack on the island in 1942, and the squadron subsequently disbanded to reform in the UK during February that year, with Avro Lancasters which were used in night raids on Germany until the end of the war. Re-equipped with Avro Lincoln the squadron moved to Malaya in 1950 to participate in Operation *Firedog* against the communist terrorist, returning to the UK in 1954, to convert to EE Canberra B. 2s. These were operated by the squadron until 1959, when it stood down, to be re-activated in 1962, with Handley Page Victors as part of the nuclear deterrent "V" Force. Disbanded again in 1968, the squadron re-appeared in the 1972 battle order as a target facilities unit with TT. 18s (Target Tugs) based at RAF West Raynham, Norfolk. Following the decision to centralise the remaining EE Canberra fleet at RAF Wyton the squadron moved there in January 1982, having previously spent four years at Marham. Following the withdrawal of all EE Canberra variants excepting the PR 7/PR 9s the squadron re-equipped with the BAe Hawk for target facility duties in September 1991 at RAF Finningley, Yorks.

Closure of the Finningley base forced a further move to the Tornado ADV base at RAF Leeming, North Yorks on 21 September 1995. This was a logical move in as much as the squadron spends much of its time flying as radar decoys for the training of Tornado F 3 WISOs on the A.I. 24 Foxhunter radar. For this task to enhance the returns on the F 3s TV Tabulator Displays some of No.100s Hawks have been fitted with a special under fuselage radar 'exciter' unit as the Hawks normal radar signature presented the trainee radar operators with identification difficulties. Further, since establishing at Leemimg No.100 Squadron has acquired additional aircraft to undertake the training of FAC (Forward Air Control) crews.

No. 100 Squadrons 'Gloss Black' BAe Hawks provide A.I 24Foxhunter radar 'targeting' for the F3 Tornado fleet

Aircraft Markings and Codes

As might be expected night-bomber units were not allocated unit markings in the First World War, so none of the squadrons airplanes carried markings of any sort. As neither did the Bristol Fighters used in Ireland, although it is thought Airco D. H. 9s used later, did carry individual numbers for identification. Fairey Fawns also carried individual numbers, changed to squadron numbering just before the squadron received Hawker Horsley bombers. These airplanes had '100' painted forward of the roundel with an individual aircraft letter aft, while the Vildebeest torpedo-bombers carried an unofficial badge as depicted or a 'skull and crossbones' emblem on the fin for a time, but later as the war in the Pacific took hold only individual aircraft numbers and serials were carried.

Unofficial Badge

Following the Munich Crisis of 1938, the official code letters RA- were allocated and applied to Vildebeest, the code changed to NK- in September, 1939. On rejoining Bomber Command the squadrons Avro Lancasters were allocated the official code HW- and this was carried over to the post-war Avro Lincolns until July 1951, when squadron identification was reduced to the colour of the propeller spinners, green on No.100 Squadron's airplanes. In March 1952, enlarged serials were repeated aft of the fuselage roundel. And a small squadron badge was usually carried beneath the cockpit side windows. The arrival at RAF Wittering of EE Canberra jet bombers saw gold and blue chequered fins denoting the base's association with the Borough of Stamford. No. 100 Squadron airplanes superimposed a unit badge on a green disc, but airplanes detached to Wyton and Christmas Island usually had red fins with a white "skull and crossbones" on a green disc displayed. H. P. Victors retained this badge on the fin, toned down to a pale blue or red disc with a white emblem on anti-flash nuclear deterrent airplanes. The blue and gold checks re-appeared later on the fins of the squadron's Canberra TT 18s with the squadron badge in a green disc superimposed on them. some of the airplanes also had the Stamford Coat of Arms on the front fuselage, but this was subsequently deleted with the units re-location to Wyton, Hunts, in January 1982. Two letter squadron identification codes having been introduced in November 1981, No. 100 using prefix 'C'.

Conversion to BAe Hawks in 1993, saw the airplanes in low-viz European grey camouflage with the blue and gold chequers displayed high on the fin surmounted by the two letter identification code in white, with the squadron 'skull and crossbones' superimposed on a blue and gold chequered edged 'squared diamond' below the pilots cockpit.

No. 7 Squadron

RAF Odiham, Hants. Army Support. (JHC)
Boeing Vertol Chinook HC 2 (18) HC 3 (8 - 2003)
& Westland Gazelle AH 1 (1)
Motto : *Per diem, per noctem* — 'By day and by night

Formed at on 1 May 1914, at South Farnborough, Hants, No. 7 Squadron served as a Corps reconnaissance unit but in the inter-war period gained fame as a bomber squadron operating Vickers Vimy, Virginia and A. W. Whitley airplanes. It was the first RAF unit to receive Short Stirling bombers whose wing-span was dictated by the size of the hangars available at the time. In WW II No. 7 Squadron was assigned to night bombing operations, retaining it Stirlings until July 1943, when it received Avro Lancasters. The post-war era saw a continuation in the bomber role initially with Avro Lincoln and latterly with Vickers Valiant, the first of the RAF's V-bomber fleet. Following disbandment in September, 1962 it was not until May 1970, that the squadron reformed at RAF St Mawgan as a target facilities unit with Canberra TT. 18. After disbanding again in 1981 the squadron reformed at RAF Odiham, Hants, in September, 1982 to become the first Chinook squadron and the type have been operated by the squadron ever since. In 1983/84, the squadron was called upon to operate its Chinooks in the Middle East, for a period, when it was deployed to Akrotiri, Cyprus, in support of British Forces in the Lebanon. On the 1 May 1989, No.7 Squadron, celebrated its 75th anniversary since it was one of the last RFC Squadrons to be formed on 1 May 1914. In January 1991, No. 7 Squadron supplied helicopters and crews to help form the Joint Helicopter Support Unit in the Gulf along with crews and aircraft from No.18 Squadron. Based at Ras ali Ghar, Saudia Arabia the Composite "Chinook" Squadron Middle East, lifted over 1,000,000 kilos of freight in the first seven weeks of operations. More recently No.7 Squadron deployed to Bosnia, with four of its Chinook H.C.2 to join the Laarbruch detachment of the Implementation Force (IFOR).

Currently the squadron operates the updated (all H.C.1 conversions) H.C.2 (CH-47D) variant to which it started to convert in 1993. Early 1999 saw No.7 Squadron on the front-line again supplying Chinook heavylift helicopters in support of NATO KFOR operations in Kosovo.

No. 7 Squadron operates a single Westland Gazelle AH 1.

Aircraft Markings and Codes

Aircraft markings were first applied to No. 7 Squadron aircraft in 1916, when two coloured bands were placed around the rear fuselage close to the tailplane. Black on clear doped airplanes and white on the Khaki drab B.E. 2cs. R. E. 8s had two white bands on the fuselage well forward of the fin.

In 1923, the squadron's Vickers Vimy were initially unmarked except for a black "7" in a white circle on the sides of the nose. Vickers Virginia were similarly marked until dark green (Nivo) night camouflage was applied in 1926. After which individual white letters on a black panel were painted on the nose and rear fuselage. some of the aircraft also had the name of a star on the nose. Similar variations of these markings were used throughout the 1930s, including an unofficial squadron badge on the tip of the nose of some airplanes. A. W. Whitleys carried the figure "7" on the side of the fuselage near the roundel with an individual letter on the other side.

Unofficial Badge

After the Munich Crisis the official unit code LT- replaced the figure "7" , changing to MG- in September, 1939, appearing on Short Stirling bombers in a uniquely small size. The MG- code was used again after the war on Avro Lancasters and Lincolns until 1951, when all codes were removed and squadron's identity reduced to a badge positioned under the pilot's cockpit side windows. Propeller spinners were painted "blue" donating No. "7" Squadron.

In 1952, Bomber Command started using enlarged airplane serials on the fuselage sides. Victor Valiants displayed the centre portion of the squadron badge (seven white stars of the constellation Ursa Major - "Great Bear") on a blue disc background on the tail-fin. These markings being retained on the EE Canberra TT 18s and the Boeing Vertol CH-47 Chinooks which also have two-letter unit airplane codes in black on the rear rotor mounting.

No. 7 Squadron Chinook

No. 7 Squadron Chinook with load

63.

No. 18 Squadron

RAF Odiham, Hants.   Air Transport (Army) (JHC)
Boeing Vertol Chinook HC 2/HC 2A (6)
Motto : *Animo et fide* — 'With courage and faith'

Since its formation at Northolt, North London, on 11 May 1915, No. 18 Squadron has undertaken a considerable variety of tasks ranging from fighter reconnaissance through strategic bombing to transport. First established as a fighter reconnaissance unit, the squadron was originally equipped with the Vickers F.B. 5 Gunbus and F. E. 2b but the unit soon switched to the bombing role with Airco D. H. 4 day bombers. Disbanded at the end of WW I the squadron did not reform until 1931, initially with the superb Hawker Hart biplane bomber followed by Hinds from the same stable and then Blenheims from the Bristol company. With the latter the squadron saw action in North Africa in WW II but by the time it moved north to Italy it was equipped with the more capable American Douglas Boston light-bombers. Post-WW II duties included a short spell as a Douglas C-47 (C.4) Dakota transport unit before it resumed bombing duties with EE Canberras and Vickers Valiants until disbanding in March, 1963. Reforming in January 1964, the squadron equipped with Westland Wessex HC 2 helicopters for Army Support duties, converting to the twin-rotor Boeing Vertol Chinook in August 1981. During 1992 while based at Laarbruch, the squadron supplemented its Chinooks with five Westland/Aerospatiale Puma 1s.

In February 1994, No.18 Squadron began to receive, upgraded Boeing (CH-47D) H.C.2s (converted H.C.1s), of which they took four to Bosnia on 8 January 1996, as part of the Implementation Force (IFOR). The squadron returned to Odiham on the 1 April 1997, having relinquished its Puma Flight to No.72 Squadron in Northern Ireland in March 1997. Currently No.18 Squadron remains operational with its Chinook H.C.2s at RAF Odiham having returned to the UK from Laarbruch at the end of 1999. Since when the squadron had been operational in Sierra Leone and more recently (2002), in support of 45 Commando Royal Marines deployment in Afghanistan in the war against terrorism. One of the squadrons most renowned operations in modern times was in 1982, in the South Atlantic, when the sole survivor of a four ship detachment, following the sinking of the *Atlantic Conveyor* performed truly outstanding feats in support of the re-occupation of the islands, often carrying loads far in excess of the manufacturers recommended safe operating parameters.

Aircraft Markings and Codes

No unit markings were carried on the squadrons airplanes in WW I until it re-roled as a day bomber unit with Airco D. H. 4s. These airplanes carried a white square aft of the fuselage roundel and an airplane identification letter or number, with this individual marking repeated on the bombers upper wing centre section of the Flight Leaders airplane. Silver painted Hawker Harts flown in the 1930s carried an '18' forward of the fuselage roundel and some had a 'Pegasus' badge on the fin. Hawker Hinds had similar markings, a few also carried a version of the squadron badge on the fin.

Unofficial Badge

It is believed early Bristol Blenheim airplanes may have displayed an '18' until the Munich Crisis of 1938, gave rise the official GU- code although it is not known whether this was displayed. From 1939, the official code WV- was used until the unit was deployed to the Mediterranean theatre where both Blenheim and Boston airplanes carried only individual identification letters, as did the post-war Avro Lancaster and D. H. Mosquitos.

Transport Command Douglas Dakotas carried no unit markings as with centralised servicing the airplanes were drawn from a pool as and when required. But in August 1953, silver-painted EE Canberra target tugs carried a black 'speedbird' insignia on each side of the nose, and later carried a red 'Pegasus' badge on the tip-tanks. When the squadron moved to RAF Upwood in December 1956, the Station Shield was displayed on the fin. Vickers Valiant B 1s were unmarked except for a red 'Pegasus' on a light blue disc painted on the fin, and the Westland Wessex helicopters continued to display this emblem, although during the general tone down of all RAF airplane markings in the 1970s the white disc was changed to black. Also during 1970, two-letter codes were introduced, 'B' denoting No. 18 Squadron as the suffix to the individual airplane letter. Boeing Vertol Chinooks carry the same basic markings on the rear rotor mounting, the 'Pegasus' displayed in red on a blue disc, and the two-letter code in black, is repeated on the front of the forward rotor mounting.

A well-worn No 18 Squadron airplane on army support operations. Note angle of blade 'droop' on forward rotor assembly   (RAF)

No. 27 Squadron
RAF Odiham, Hants. Army Support and OC Flight. (JHC)
Boeing Vertol Chinook HC 2 (10)
Motto : *Quam celerrime ad astra* -'With all speed to the Stars'

Formed on 5 November, 1915, at Hounslow, the squadron's association with the Martinsyde G100 'Elephant', being the only squadron to fully equip with the type, and its long stay in India, gave rise to the adoption of the 'elephant' as the unofficial and later the official unit badge. Airco D. H. 4 and D. H. 9 day bombers were used by the squadron for bombing operations in France in WW I until the squadron disbanded in January, 1920. A few months later No. 99 Squadron was re-numbered No. 27 Squadron to fly patrols over the North West Frontier of India with Westland Wapiti until the outbreak of WW II. The squadron then became a training unit but later received Bristol Blenheims and went to Malaya as a night fighter unit, unfortunately losing all of its airplanes in the Japanese invasion. Although the squadron remained in the Far East to fly Bristol Beaufighters and later D. H. Mosquito fighter-bombers until disbanded in 1946.

In 1947, No. 27 Squadron reformed in the UK as a transport unit with Douglas Dakota C-47s taking part in the Berlin airlift. Re-equipment with EE Canberra light-bombers in 1953, saw a return to offensive operations and it remained in this role after moving to RAF Scampton, Lincs, in 1961, as part of the V-Force equipped with Avro Vulcan B. 2. Operating in the maritime radar reconnaissance role with the Vulcan SR. 2 variant throughout the 1970s. Returning to overland strike/attack duties on moving to RAF Marham, Norfolk, where it received Panavia Tornado GR 1s in August 1983. Deployments to the Middle East and successes in the SAC Bombing and Navigation Competition in the United States in 1985, were followed by No.27 operating out of Marham as part of No.1 Group, Strike Command, with the unit relinquishing its Tornado GR.1s to No.12 Squadron on 1 October 1993, for operation in the maritime strike role. On the same day the famous "Elephant " badge was handed to No.240 OCU at RAF Odiham the unit becoming No.27 (Reserve) Squadron, equipped with six Chinook HC.1 and five Westland/Aerospatiale Puma HC.1s for Army Support and training of relevant crews. Similar duties are still undertaken today (2002), No.27 Squadron now operating solely the upgraded Boeing/Vertol (CH-47D) HC 2 Chinook, its Pumas having joined No.33 Squadron in February 1998.

As well as having responsibility to train all the RAF's Chinook crews, in 1999, No. 27 Squadron was deployed aboard the Royal Navy's helicopter assault ship HMS *Ocean* for shipboard compatibility trials, as part of the newly formed Joint Helicopter Command (JHC). More recent front-line operations were undertaken in the mountains of Afghanistan in support of the British Marine Commando operations in 2002.

Aircraft markings and codes.

Official unit markings were not carried on the squadron's G100 Elephants, some carried individual airplane identification letters — large numerals painted on the sides of the engine cowlings. Most of the airplanes also had a small wooden shield on the forward fuselage on which was painted an 'elephant' symbol.

Unofficial Badge

No. 27 Sqdn.

Post-war the squadron Airco D. H. 9 day bombers carried code letters in white on a black square aft of the fuselage roundel but sometimes on the engine cowling and occasionally on the top wing surfaces. Later airplanes carried a '27' painted in black on the fin, but in the late 1920s an emerald green 'elephant' badge was carried instead. Westland Wapitis, had the airplane letter forward on the engine cowling, and there was a red band painted around the fuselage just forward of the tail unit, and a green 'elephant' was carried on the fin superimposed on a white grenade-shaped shield.

Following the Munich Crisis, the official code MY- was allocated but probably not carried, until changed to PT- in September 1939, to be carried on Bristol Blenheims in Malaya. Bristol Beaufighters and D. H. Mosquitos carried individual aircraft letters but no unit markings, the jungle rescue Beaufighters also carried SEAC identification stripes across the wings, tailplane, fin and rudder. No unit markings were displayed on the squadrons Dakota transports and at first the Canberra bombers had only a red 'Speedbird' on the nose, but later the Scampton stripe was added running the whole length of the fuselage. Initially the all-over white anti-flash Avro Vulcans carried a small squadron badge on each side of the nose, but by the time the 'Blue Steel' equipped airplanes were on strength the green 'elephant' was displayed on the fin, and the badge was re-positioned on the fuselage immediately aft of the roundel. On camouflaged Avro Vulcans the badge was deleted, but on the strategic reconnaissance airplanes the 'elephant' on the fin appeared on a white disc. Panavia Tornado carried more flamboyant markings with the green 'elephant' on a yellow disc superimposed on a red stripe on the airplanes RWR casing. A yellow-rimmed green arrow head is carried on the nose, with the individual two-numeral identification code displayed in green outlined in yellow forward high on the fin below the RWR casing. Boeing-Vertol Chinooks have the units badge on the rear rotor housing, a dark green elephant on a green circle, flanked by green and dark green stripes. Two-letter individual airplane identification letters are displayed in black towards the rear of the housing.

A Westland/Aerospatiale Puma HC 1 of No. 27 Squadron displaying the 'elephant' badge on the forward fuselage cabin door

No. 33 Squadron

RAF Benson, Oxon. Army Support and OC Flight (JHC)
Westland/Aerospatiale Puma HC 1 (15)
Motto : *Loyalty*

No. 33 Squadron was formed on 12 January, 1916, as a Home Defence and training unit. Responsible for the Midlands anti-Zeppelin patrols, in reality the squadron saw little action in WW I. In 1929, it became a light-bomber unit with Hawker Horsleys and later, Hawker Harts which it took to Egypt in 1935,before receiving Gloster Gladiator biplane fighters in February 1938, these succeeded by Hawker Hurricanes in September 1940.

During WW II it served as a fighter unit in the Mediterranean before returning to the UK to re-equip with Supermarine Spitfires in 1944, these replaced by Hawker Tempest when the squadron became part of the 2nd TAF. Post-war still equipped with Tempests, the squadron was dispatched to the Far East but later re-equipped with D. H. Hornet for operation in Malaya.

On returning to the UK, the squadron specialised in night-fighter operations initially with D. H. Venom NF. 2s, then A. W. Meteor NF 14 finally receiving Gloster Javelin all-weather night-fighters in July, 1958, becoming a Bloodhound 2 SAM unit for five years. The squadron was resurrected again at RAF Odiham on 14 June 1971, as the first Westland/Aerospatiale Puma HC 1 unit, to provide additional support for No.38 Groups Rapid Reaction Force. No. 33 Squadron still operates it upgraded tactical support helicopters today, more than a quarter of a century later, having relocated to RAF Benson on 13 September 1997, having assimilated No.18 Squadrons flight of five Pumas into its inventory.

During the NATO KFOR operations in April 1999, two of the squadrons Pumas supported the Army's No. 4 Armoured Brigade in the medevac of refugees crossing to Macedonia from Kosovo. Throughout 1999/2000 the squadron based two Puma HC 1s at Pristina Airport, as part of the Kosovo KFOR+ deployment within Operation *Joint Guard*. Currently (2002) No. 33 Squadron remains at RAF Benson with its Puma HC 1 tasked with tactical army support.

No. 33 Squadron Puma on operations over the English countryside

68.

Aircraft Markings and Codes

The squadrons airplanes carried no markings in WW I as it was not customary for Home Defence units to do so. On reforming as a day bomber unit, the squadrons Hawker Horsleys had the numerals '33' painted on the fuselage forward of the roundels and some airplanes carried a black band aft. The '33' marking was carried over to Hawker Harts, the numerals placed above the roundel and painted in Flight colours, 'B' Flights outlined in black. Later the Hart emblem was displayed in black on the fin with a small '33' underneath. While detached to the Middle East for the Abyssinian Crisis, no unit markings were carried but on being redesignated a fighter unit the squadron badge was applied to the fins of the Gloster Gladiators in a standard white 'spearhead'.

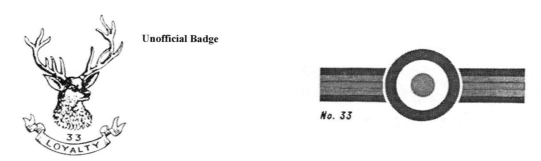

Unofficial Badge

No. 33

The allocation of official codes following the Munich Crisis, saw No. 33 Squadron display SO- on its airplanes aft of the fuselage roundel with an individual airplane letter forward. The 'spearhead' symbol was subsequently removed when the Gladiators were camouflaged. It is thought the SO- code was used by mistake by the squadron as in April 1939, this changed to TN- and following the outbreak of war to NW- which was carried on the Hawker Hurricane operated during the early Desert and Greek operations. Although from mid-1941 until the squadron returned to the UK in 1944, no unit markings were carried. Except from January to June 1943 on re-equipping with Supermarine Spitfires the RS- code was used. On return to the UK in April 1944, official code 5R- was carried until mid-1953, when it was removed from the squadrons D. H. Hornets. Then a number of different coloured markings were tried on the Hornets until the squadron settled on pale blue rectangles edged top and bottom in dark blue each side of the fuselage roundel. Individual airplane letters were also applied to the rear fuselage in white. These same markings were applied to D. H. Venom night fighters, with individual airplane letters applied to the nose-wheel door, in red for 'A' Flight and blue for 'B' Flight. A. W. Meteor NF 14s were similarly marked but with the code letter also applied to the fin. Gloster Javelin all-weather night fighters saw the squadron colours painted across the top of the fin and rudder just below the fin-top tailplane, while the airplane code pale blue outlined in the Flight colour, was placed between the nose mounted roundel and the engine air intake. When Javelin FAW 9s replaced the FAW 7s a pale blue disc mounting a black Hart's head was superimposed on the tail stripe and the individual letter was moved to the fin. Puma helicopters initially carried the Hart's head emblem flanked by blue/red bars on the starboard cockpit door, and the unit code 'C' painted in black on the tail boom together with the airplanes individual identification letter. Later the Hart's head emblem was displayed on the fuselage sides beneath the cockpit windows.

No. 230 Squadron
RAF Aldergrove, Northern Ireland. Tactical Support (JHC)
Westland Puma/Aerospatiale HC 1 (18)
Motto : *Kita chari jauh* - (Malay) 'We seek far'

Formed on 20 August 1918, at Felixstowe, Suffolk, for a short time until the Armistice in November, 1918, No. 230 Squadron was deployed using flying-boats for North Sea patrols. Retained post-war until April 1923, with Felixstowe F. 2as, F. 5s and Fairey IIIC Seaplanes until April 1923. Reformed in December 1934, again as a flying-boat unit the squadron operated Short Singapore from Egypt in 1935, and the returned briefly to the UK before departing for Singapore in 1937. Re-equipment with the Short Sunderland followed in 1938, and this marked the start of a long association with the type, which remained in use with the squadron until it disbanded in February, 1957. Throughout the Sunderland era, the squadron flew operations from a number of diverse locations including Singapore, Ceylon, Egypt, Burma, Tanganyika, the Mediterranean and the UK.

In 1958, No. 215 Squadron was re-numbered No. 230 Squadron to operate Scottish Pioneer, and Twin Pioneers light transports on army support and communications duties before becoming a helicopter unit with Westland Whirlwind HAR 10 in June 1962. Some two years was spent in Germany followed by a move to Borneo in February 1965. No. 230 Squadron returned to the UK in late 1966 and retained the Whirlwind until re-equipped with Westland/Aerospatiale Puma HC 1 in November 1971. Following a spell in Germany with the reduction in British Forces in the country, during 1992 No. 230 Squadron was re-located to RAF Aldergrove, Northern Ireland, in support of British Army operations in the province. The squadron is still retained on this deployment more than a decade later in 2002.

No. 230 "Tiger" Squadron

Aircraft markings and codes

In WW I flying-boats operating from Felixstowe were painted in a number of bizarre colour schemes although squadron markings were not carried. Short Singapores received post-war were also unmarked, except for an individual letter in black on the hull beneath the cockpit windows. Following the Munich Crisis the official code FV- was allocated to the unit but as with most other squadrons almost certainly was not carried on the Singapores or the Sunderland replacements. From September 1939, the official code was changed to NM- which was used until the unit left for East Africa in early 1943. For the remainder of the war the Sunderlands only carried individual letters, but on return to home shores in 1946 the code 4X- was introduced and a unit badge appeared on the side of the forward hull. In 1951, the single code B- replaced the 4X-, later dropped in favour of the squadron '230' number. This was painted in black forward of the hull roundel with the airplanes individual ident letter aft.

Scottish Pioneers carried a single airplane letter identification on the rear fuselage, this being moved onto the fins of the Twin Pioneers that followed and later on Whirlwind helicopters appeared on the boom. Whirlwinds also had a black five-sided shield painted on the forward fuselage with a tiger head and the numerals '230' on the head in yellow. Westland Pumas saw the introduction of a two-letter code, the airplanes individual letter prefixed by the unit identification 'D', painted on the tail boom forward of the roundel above the UHF radio antenna. The squadron badge was painted on a turquoise disc on the main cabin doors, and the 'palm tree' light green and the 'tiger' yellow and black. A white and gold tiger has been used on occasion, especially when the aircraft have been prepared with 'tiger stripes' for participation in the NATO 'Tiger Meets'. Current (2002) unit markings feature a 'tiger' in front of a palm tree on a black pentagon.

The demise of No. 74(F) "Tiger" Squadron has seen No. 230 Squadron take up the Tiger mantle, having attended a number of NATO "Tiger Meets" suitably adorned

71.

No. 28 Squadron

RAF Benson, Oxon, Tactical Support (JHC)
EHI Merlin HC 3 (18)
Motto : *Quicquid agas age* — Whatever you may do, do'

No. 28 Squadron formed at Gosport, Hants, in November 1915, and then served on the Italian Front equipped with Sopwith Camels. Post-war the squadron moved to India's North West Frontier where it flew Westland Wapitis and Hawker Harts. During WW II the squadron saw service in Burma with Westland Lysanders, Supermarine Spitfires and rocket-firing Hawker Hurricane IIs mostly on reconnaissance duties. After the war the squadron took up residence at Hong Kong, remaining there to fly successively Supermarine Spitfires, D. H. Vampire and Venom fighter-bombers, Hawker Hunter FGA 9s, Westland Whirlwind HAR 10s and then Westland Wessex HC 2.

Having moved to Sek Kong in June 1978. An important detachment to South Australia occurred in September 1987 which involved the squadron in Operation *Maralinga*. The aircraft had flown to Australia on a four month detachment to take part in the radiological survey of the old atomic bomb test sites, most of which had previously been used by the UK for testing V-bomber nuclear weapons. Having flown the Westland Wessex HC.2 throughout the whole of the types operational life, the squadron disbanded on 30 June 1997, with a final flight around the Provence having been undertaken on 3 June before the six remaining aircraft were handed over to the Uruguayan Air Force and Hong Kong was handed back to the Chinese. No. 28 Squadron having served exclusively overseas for over 77 years, of which 48 had been spent in Hong Kong.

No.28 Squadron reformed at RAF Benson, Oxon, in September 1999, as the first operator of the RAF's new general purpose helicopter the Westland/Agusta EH101 Merlin HC.3. The squadron returning to carry out its tasks from home soils for the first time since early 1919, after almost eighty years continuous overseas service..!

Merlin HC 3 Tactical Support Helicopters equip the reformed No. 28 Squadron

Aircraft Markings and Codes

The official unit marking allocated for display on No. 28 Squadrons Sopwith Camel was a white square aft of the fuselage roundel, and this was used in France and Italy, though often it was supplanted by multiple white bands around the rear fuselage whilst the squadron was based in Italy. Individual airplane letters were usually painted in white forward of the roundel, and after the Armistice in November 1918, individual experienced pilots were allowed their own colour schemes.

In 1920, in India the Bristol Fighters carried no unit markings, with only a single individual airplane letter painted in black aft of the roundel. Westland Wapiti replacements just over a decade later featured a black fuselage top decking and a black band immediately forward of the tailplane. Hawker Audax were similarly marked and also a squadron emblem was painted on the fin within a six-pointed star. Following the Munich Crisis the official code US- was allocated and carried forward of the fuselage roundel, the individual airplane identification letter being moved aft. The black band was removed at this time, but silver-painted Hawker Audax displayed the squadron emblem on the fin. In September 1939, the units official code was changed to BF- and as the squadrons Lysanders were slowly camouflaged the codes were applied in light-grey colour.

Hawker Hurricane IIs carried SEAC markings in mid-1943 and code marking reverted to a single letter aft of the roundel. White identification stripes were painted on the wings, tailplane, fin and the rudder. Supermarine Spitfires were similarly marked, although post-war a few airplanes also carried a squadron emblem on the fin. Introduction of D. H. Vampire fighter-bombers in February 1951, brought more colourful markings. These consisted of dark-blue bars outlined in yellow on each side of the boom roundel. Hawker Hunter day fighters retained the bar markings, which were moved to the nose and flanked by a white disc on which was painted the squadron 'winged horse'.

Westland Whirlwind helicopters carried a squadron badge on the tail rotor pylon and a single white code letter on the aft fuselage sides, while on the Wessex the markings reverted to a tail-mounted emblem, the 'winged horse' , in red on a blue background outlined in yellow. Individual aircraft identification letters were retained on the rear fuselage which also carried broad white bands. EHI Merlin HC 3 are to carry a 'winged horse' above two white crosses on a red shield. (as denoted on the squadron badge which interestingly represents the White Horse on the downs near Yatesbury, Wilts, which was the squadron's first operational base).

Italian MMI 'Merlin'

73.

No. 78 Squadron

RAF Mount Pleasant, Falkland Islands. Transport/SAR
Westland Sea King HAR 3 (2)
Boeing Vertol Chinook HC 2 (1)
Motto : *Nemo non paratus* - 'Nobody unprepared'

No. 78 Squadron was formed at Newhaven on 1 November, 1916, as a night fighter squadron for Home Defence duties based in the south of England, to combat the Zeppelin and Gotha bomber raids. Converted from Sopwith 1½ Strutters to Camels and then Snipes before disbanding on 31 December, 1919. It reformed as a A. W. Whitley bomber squadron in November 1936, but worked as a Group Pool Unit training new crews until July, 1940. Converting to the Handley Page Halifax in March, 1942, as a night-bombing unit and flew in this role through the night-bomber offensive against Germany until the wars end. Post-war it became a transport unit with Douglas Dakota C.4 operating in the Mediterranean and the Middle East. The Dakotas were replaced by Vickers Valettas in 1950, and the Scottish Pioneer in 1956, in support of the Army in Aden.

In October 1958, No. 78 Squadron re-equipped with the larger Twin Pioneer C.C.2s, with detachments to Firq in Muscat and Sharjah in the Trucial Oman in support of the Sultan of Omans armed forces. At this time an attempt was made to provide the "Twin Pins" with some kind of self defence, by way of a Bren-gun mounted in the rear entrance and Nord SS 11 wire-guided missiles fitted on racks under the wings, with trials completed in 1962. Interestingly the following year, a No. 78 Squadron "Twin Pin" fired off a missile against rebel forces, and it is thought that this was the first ever operational missile firing by the RAF - achieved by a light-transport unit..! While still in Aden, in June 1965, the squadron received its first rotary-winged aircraft by way of the Westland Wessex HC 2 helicopter, moving to Sharjah in October 1967 on closure of the Aden base for support work with the Trucial States. On 1 December 1971, with the complete withdrawal of British Forces from the Middle East, the squadron was disbanded.

Fifteen years later on 22 May 1986, No.78 Squadron was reformed at RAF Mount Pleasant in the Falkland Islands by combining No.1310 (Tactical Support) Flight and No. 1564 (Tactical Support) Flight with Chinook helicopters and Sea King helicopters respectively into a single No.78 Squadron. Which remains the situation today, with the unit tasked with Army Support and heavy lift with its Boeing Vertol Chinook HC 2s, and SAR and maritime reconnaissance with its Westland Sea King HAR 3s.

Aircraft markings and codes.
No unit markings were carried on No. 78 Squadrons airplanes in WW I. H. P. Heyfords carried individual airplane letters. The first type to carry unit markings were the A. W. Whitley bombers, initially just the squadron number on the fuselage forward of the roundel, changed to the official YY- code following the Munich Crisis of 1938. With the issue of new wartime codes, No 78 Squadron used EY- from September 1939 onwards, with the same code carried on H. P. Halifaxes and, quite unusually on the squadrons Douglas Dakota transports flown in the Middle East.

By the time Vickers Valetta C. 1 transports entered service in April 1950, unit code letters had been dropped on Middle East Air Force transports and the squadrons airplanes were only distinguishable by their red propeller spinners. No squadron markings were carried on the units light-transport planes in Aden until Westland Wessex HC 2 helicopters were taken on charge in June 1965, when a large squadron badge was displayed on the main cabin door and a white aircraft identification letter was painted aft of the fuselage roundel.

In the Falklands, a yellow 'tiger' with two tails on a black disc is painted on the tail rotor mounting of the Chinooks, together with an aircraft letter, and by the cockpit on the Sea King HAR 3s.

No. 84 Squadron

RAF Akrotiri, Cyprus. Comunications and SAR
Westland Wessex HC 2C (3) (March 2003 civil Bell 412s)
Motto : *Scorpiones pungunt* — 'Scorpions sting'

Unofficial Badge

No 84 Squadron formed on 7 January, 1917, as a scout unit with S. E. 5A and crossed to France in September,1917, and afterwards went to Iraq and Egypt with D. H. 9s, Westland Wapitis, Vickers Vincents and Bristol Blenheims. It took part in the Greek campaign and then the Western Desert being posted to Sumatra and then Java in the early days of the Pacific War. The squadron is unique in never having been based in the UK and now, 2002, is the first RAF squadron to have a female commanding officer. Although with only three obsolete Westland Wessex helicopters on strength due to be withdrawn in March 2003, maybe not for long, with civil-registered Bell 412s destined to replace them !

On arrival in India in WW II, the squadron flew Vultee Vengeance dive-bombers over Burma until these were replaced by D. H. Mosquito VI fighter-bombers in 1945. Post-war, after a spell in Singapore, No. 84 Squadron moved to Iraq in 1948, with Bristol Brigands and returned to Singapore to fly in support of ground forces involved in Operation *Firedog*. Flying its first strike mission on 14 April 1950. Unfortunately whilst the squadron found the aircraft extremely effective and operated it extensively to attack the terrorist, dropping bombs and rockets, it was decidedly troublesome, and after a series of accidents forced its grounding in January 1953, the squadron was disbanded at Tengah on 20 February 1953, having flown some 2,038 sorties. Its aircraft were scrapped on the spot, but on the same day at Fayid, Egypt, No.204 Squadron flying Vickers Valetta C.1 on general transport duties was redesignated No.84 squadron.

With the evacuation of the Canal Zone, and Egypt the squadron moved to Nicosia, Cyprus in March, 1956, where its newly gained experience in "para dropping" was put to good use in the Suez Campaign of November 1956. Following the conclusion of the Suez Operations, the squadron moved to the Middle East, to RAF Khormaksar, Aden, to supplement the Aden Communications Flight. The squadrons primary role was to provide support for the Army, and in June 1958 one flight converted to Blackburn Beverley C.1 tactical transports. The type proved to be well suited for the task and by August 1960 the squadron had completely re-equipped with the cavernous transport, handing its remaining Valetta C.1s over to the reformed No.233 Squadron on 1 September 1960. The squadron was responsible for the logistic support of British and South Arabian Army units in and around the Aden Peninsula. It also played an important part in the Brunei operations and by July 1963 the squadrons Beverleys had flown some 2 million miles conveying over 60,000 passengers and 20,000 tons of freight. Whilst operating from the Khormaksar base the squadron made regular re-supply flights to the up-country airstrip at Thumier in the Radfan Mountains, the squadrons XH121 being the first Beverley transport to land on the specially lengthened runway to accommodate the type. Seven years later, the Beverleys were replaced by H.S. Andover C.1s and the unit moved to RAF Sharjah for operations with the Trucial Oman Scouts, where it remained until returning to RAF Muharraq, Bahrain, for disbandment on 31 October 1971.

However, within months No. 84 Squadron reformed at RAF Akrotiri, Cyprus, by renumbering No.1563 (SAR) Flight with Westland Whirlwind HAR 10s helicopters and absorbing a detachment of No.230 Squadron who were on the island operating with the United Nations peace-keeping force. The squadron continued with the Whirlwind HAR 10s until one flight re-equipped with Westland Wessex HC.2 in March 1982, with "B" Flight detached at Nicosia receiving ex-FAA Wessex HU-5s in 1984. With the rest of the squadron at Akrotiri, re-equipped with HU-5s during 1985.

The squadron continues with its tasks at Akrotiri, until today, and is still multi-tasked, supplementing its SAR duties with re-supply duties, supporting the UN control posts in the Kyrenia mountain range. In 1984, the squadron played an important role during the Lebanese Crisis, evacuating members of the UN peace-keeping force from the beleaguered city of Beirut. The squadrons rather aged Wessex HU 5s continued to operate from the base at Akrotiri, for another ten years when having been supplanted by Wessex HC.2s in November 1994, the HU 5s were finally withdrawn from use in February 1995.

Currently (2002), the squadron (rather unusually) commanded by a female Squadron Leader still operates three Westland Wessex HC.2s in the SAR/Support role at Akrotiri, thus maintaining Britains presence on the island, at the Sovereign base, which is also used for regular detachments by Panavia F.3 Tornados for APC (Armament Practice Camp), and the Red Arrows aerobatic team for "winter" practicing, and transiting aircraft on Middle East detachments, to Saudi Arabia, and operations over Iraq.

Aircraft markings and codes.

With the squadron reaching the Western Front in September, 1917, its S. E. 5As carried a white horizontal stripe along the fuselage sides and on the top decking aft of the roundel. The following year, this changed to two white bars painted one each side of the fuselage and sloping inwards at the top. The first Airco D. H. 9 day- bombers carried only a unit letter, but gradually Flight symbols were introduced, playing card, 'Aces' for 'A' Flight, 'swastikas' for 'B' Flight and 'coloured triangles' for 'C' Flight. Flight motifs were also painted on Westland Wapiti general purpose airplanes, which also carried the 'scorpion' on the fin, with coloured wheel centres used to indicate the Flight.

Camouflaged Bristol Blenheims were allocated post-Munich Crisis official markings, UR-, but it is believed not carried. The official wartime VA- code was carried until the squadron was made non-operational in January, 1942. On reformation in India, only airplane letter identification was used until almost at the end of the war the squadrons D. H. Mosquitos started carrying the official PY-code painted on the rear fuselage. Replacement Bristol Beaufighter TF Xs were unmarked and the Brigands reverted to the pre-war playing card symbols, displayed on the fins in a white square, with the squadron badge appearing on the nose. Some Vickers Valetta transports also carried the 'playing card' symbol, but most were in standard Transport Command livery, with black-painted propeller spinners identifying the squadron. Blackburn Beverley transports retained the 'card' symbol on the fins and a large 'scorpion' emblem on the nose. The markings retained when the airplanes were camouflaged. Initially HS Andovers only carried the squadron badge, on a white disc at the top of the fin, but it was not long before the playing card emblem reappeared on the all-yellow search-and-rescue Whirlwind helicopters of 'A' Flight, while camouflaged UNICYF helicopters carried 'UN' in white on a light-blue fuselage band in addition to a United Nations badge. Westland Wessex 2s were similarly marked, depending on the allocated role, but the camouflaged HU 5s in addition to a fuselage roundel superimposed on a narrow light-blue band, carried a 'scorpion' on the nose and the 'playing card' symbol on the tail rotor mounting. Currently (2002) the remaining Wessex HC 2s carry a 'scorpion' on a 'playing card', symbol (diamonds, clubs etc), with a vertical blue stripe through the roundel on the fuselage.

Westland Wessex of No. 72 Squadron, taken on inventory in August 1964, a handful still in use when the unit disbanded in April 2002

No. 60® Squadron Wessex HC2. The unit now operates Bell Griffin H.T.1 (Bell 412) at RAF Shawbury DHFS

Westland Wessex HC. 2
No. 84 Squadron Wessex

No. 1312 Flight

RAF Mount Pleasant, Falkland Islands.
BAC VC 10K (1) (det No. 101 Squadron) Flight Refuelling
Lockheed Hercules C 1P (1) (det Lyneham Transport Wing)

No Badge

No. 1312 (Transport) Flight originally formed on 19 April, 1944, at Llandow, with two Avro Anson I airplanes, until disbanding again on 21 July, 1944. It reformed on 14 September, 1954, at RAF Abingdon, Oxon, as No.1312 (Transport Support) Flight by redesignating the Transport Command Air Support Flight equipped with two Handley Page Hastings and a Vickers Valetta. The unit disbanded again on 1 April 1957 at Abingdon.

Post-Falklands War No. 1312 (In-Flight Refuelling) Flight reformed on 20 August, 1983, at Port Stanley, with three Lockheed Hercules C. 1K tankers which were withdrawn from use in 1995, supplanted by a Hercules C. 1P detached from RAF Lyneham, and a VC 10 K 4 of No. 101 Squadron from RAF Brize Norton both of which remain operational with No. 1312 Flight, at RAF Mount Pleasant today (2002).

A 'stretched' Lockheed C. 1/3P as used by No. 1312 (Refuelling/Transport) Flight in the Falklands detached from Lyneham pool

No. 2 Group

Badge : Perched on a helmet an eagle, wings expanded
Motto : "Vincenus" ("We will conquer").
Authority : Queen Elizabeth II, May, 1952.

No. 2 (Bomber) Group badge is symbolic of the Group's co-operation and close alliance with the Army. No. 2 Group was formed on 20 March 1936, at Abingdon. Disbanded on 1 March 1947, it was reformed in 1950, but disbanded on 15 November 1958. It reformed again on 1 April 1993, when RAF Germany (RAFG) was reduced to Group status within Strike Command.

Inventory (includes Reserve (R) Squadrons - OCUs) :
Boeing E-3D Sentry AEW 1 (7) — Nos. 8 and 23 (STS) Squadrons
Bombardier Global Express (5) — ASTOR *(Airborne Stand-Off Radar)* battlefield surveillance.
BAC VC 10 K1 (8) — No. 10 Squadron
Lockheed C-130J-30 Hercules C 4/C 5 (15/10) — Nos 24, 30, Plus *C4/C5 conversion flight.
Lockheed C-130 Hercules C 1/C 3 (13/16/12)— Nos 47, 57(R)*, 70
BAe 146 (2) — No. 32 (Royal) Squadron
Sikorsky S.76C Plus (1) — VVIP (Air Hanson G-XXEA)
BAe 125 CC2/CC3 (2/2)— No. 32 Squadron (Comms/VIP)
Aerospatiale AS 355F1 Twin Squirrels HCC 1 (3) — VIP supplied by Operational Support Services
EE Canberra PR. 9 (5) T. 4 (2) — No. 39 (1 PRU) Squadron
HS Nimrod R.P1 (3) — No. 51 Squadron
MDC C-17 Globemaster III (4) — No. 99 Squadron
BAC VC 10 K3 (4), K4 (5) — No. 101 Squadron
Lockheed Tristar K1 (2), KC 1 (4), C.2 (2), C.2A (1) — No. 216 Squadron

Airborne Early Warning
Detection of enemy aircraft, ships or submarines is the responsibility of the AEW and maritime patrol squadrons equipped with Boeing E-3D AEW.1 and HS Nimrod MR. 2. Linked into the UKADGE Communication and Control System are the airborne early warning aircraft with their massive Westinghouse AN/APY-2 Overland Downlook Radar (ODR), each capable of tracking up to 600 low-flying aircraft. Augmented by IFF (Identification Friend or Foe) and a sophisticated passive ESM (Electronic Support Measures) system. The E-3D carries a flight crew of five and 11 to 13 mission crew - a team of radar operators and fighter controllers and air technicians for which a new "air" brevet was created, 'AT'. This allows the airplane to operate as a flying radar station and operations centre. The Sentry provides a useful OTH (Over-The-Horizon) capability, by extending radar surveillance range beyond that afforded by ground-based radar. AEW airplanes are of great value in controlling and directing fighter planes on intercept and/or CAP missions and directing air defence fighters, but they also have a role in offensive air operations.

What might have been:
Hawker Siddeley/BAe AEW 3 Nimrod DB 3 was the ill-fated projects mission systems 'software development' airplane

What was:
Piston-engined Avro Shackleton AEW 2 descendant of the WW11 Avro Lancaster bomber

At operational altitudes the Sentry can 'see' out to 483 km (300 miles) or more, and can monitor a huge volume of airspace. Its ability to operate independently of ground-based radar makes it perfectly suited for out-of-area operations. The seven RAF Sentry airplanes, each named after the seven dwarfs are operated by Nos 8 and 23 Squadrons based at Waddington, Lincs, forming one component of the NATO-OTAN AEW Mixed Force, a multi-national force based at Gilenkirschen, Germany. No.8 Squadron is the front-line operational unit while No. 23 Squadron is the Sentry Training Squadron (STS), responsible for all training tasks, but also having an operational commitment. The aircraft carry dual markings and are pooled the respective units drawing airplanes as and when required. No.8 Squadrons markings appear on the port side and No. 23 Squadron markings appear on the starboard side. As the E-3D training unit, No. 23 Squadron runs two six-month courses each year training approximately 80 aircrew.

Formerly No. 8 Squadron had operated the obsolete piston-engined Avro Shackleton AEW Mk 2s which were used far beyond their intended retirement date due to the demise of the HS Nimrod AEW Mk 3 which was cancelled in favour of the Boeing E-3D in 1986, following radar development problems. The E-3D Sentry was declared an Initial Operational Capability (IOC) on 1 July, 1992, embodying a tremendous advance in the RAF's AEW capability.

No 8 Squadron E-3D in
80th Anniversary markings

No. 8 Squadron

RAF Waddington, Lincs. Airborne Early Warning.
Boeing E-3D Sentry (7 shared with Sentry Training Squadron)
Motto : *Uspiam et passim* - Everywhere unbounded

Formed at Brooklands in January 1915, No. 8 Squadron in WW I served in the Corps and artillery co-operation role. In 1920, the squadron moved to Iraq for policing and, in 1928 to Aden, to establish a long association with the Aden Protectorate. Where again it was involved in policing duties and operations against dissident tribesmen before, during and after WW II. Although for a short time in WW II the squadron flew bombing raids on East Africa and then maritime patrol duties, then returning to policing duties until 1967. Types used during this period include Airco D. H. 9A, Vickers Vincent, Bristol Blenheim, Vickers Wellington, D. H. Vampire and Venom fighter-bombers and latterly Hawker Hunter FGA 9 fighter-ground attack planes with which it joined with No. 43 Squadron to form the Aden Strike Wing, until moving to RAF Muharraq in the Persian Gulf in September 1967, with the closure of the Khormaksar base.

In 1972, having relocated to RAF Kinloss in the UK the squadron became the RAF's first AEW unit equipped with elderly Avro Shackleton airplanes hastily fitted out with AEW radars removed from the Royal Navy's defunct Fairey Gannet fleet. Originally intended as an interim type pending delivery of the HS/BAe Nimrod AEW 3 airplanes, subsequent radar development problems and a Government decision to purchase the Boeing E-3 Sentry airplane instead, forced the squadron to continue to operate the piston-engined Shackleton until receiving its first Boeing E-3D in mid-1991. Since having been declared an IOC (Initial Operational Capability) on 1 July 1992, the airplanes have been in constant use in all the major conflicts of the decade and for training giving rise to serious concerns as the number of airframe hours consumed. Having participated in Sky Monitor and Decisive Edge operations in support of UN airspace monitoring operations over the former Yugoslavia, flying mainly from Aviano, Italy.

In 1999/2000 No.8/23 Squadron following intense squadron activity in support of the NATO KFOR operations the squadron had two aircraft out of their inventory of six (one aircraft was out of service with a damaged wing), based at Aviano, Italy, in support of NATO forces in Bosnia and the former Republic of Yugoslavia. More recently (2002) the 'Composite' squadron has seen further intense operations in the Afghan coalition force's war against terrorism.

No. 8 Squadron Boeing E-3D Sentry in low-viz markings

83.

Aircraft Markings and Codes

Unit markings were not used on No. 8 Squadron airplanes until April 1916, when a black stripe on clear doped airplanes and a white stripe on khaki drab airplanes was painted along the top longeron from the rear cockpit to the rudder post. FK 8s carried similar markings almost always in white. Bristol Fighters were unmarked except for airplanes received from other units retained their original markings ! D. H. 9A day bombers did not initially carry unit markings only large individual airplane identification letters. However, later a large "winged 8" was painted on the rear fuselage of some airplanes.

In the mid-1920s the C.O.s airplane sported a winged emblem on the fin and centre section of the upper mainplane, while the wing and tailplane tips were painted red. Fairey IIIs also had a "winged 8" on the tail-fins during the 1920s. A decade later this had changed to a large individual airplane letter. The silver-painted Vickers Vincents also carried individual letters in Flight colours.

 **Unofficial Badge**

No. 8

After the Munich Crisis the unit code YO- was allocated, but not carried. In September 1939, the unit code changed to HV- and this was applied to the camouflaged Vincents. Bristol Blenheims were unmarked except for airplane letters on the fuselage forward of the roundel. Lockheed Hudsons were similarly marked, as were Vickers Wellington bombers until late in their service when the new unit code "A" was carried. Consolidated Liberators carried their former No. 200 Squadron airplane letter codes applied to the rear fuselage and repeated in miniature on the sides of the nose. It is probable that D. H. Mosquitos also retained their previous unit markings. Hawker Tempest saw the introduction of more distinctive and bolder markings, the aircraft carrying a large red individual code letter aft of the rear fuselage roundel, with some airplanes carrying a winged figure "8" in red on the engine cowling.

Bristol Brigand B. 1s when in standard camouflage had individual airplane codes in white immediately aft of the roundel. Later, when the fuselage sides and tops were painted white to help reduce the planes inside temperature in the Middle East theatre of operations, the airplane codes were applied in black and a squadron badge appeared on the nose. D. H. Vampires were initially unmarked until 1953, when the first "modern" colourful markings were applied by way of squadron "bars" "fish-tailed" fore and aft. D. H. Venom Is were similarly marked and the squadron badge was retained on Hawker Hunters and Avro Shackleton AEW 2s.

Whilst part of the Aden Strike Wing in the mid-1960s, before the RAF withdrew from the Middle East, Hawker Hunter FGA 9 airplanes carried dual squadron markings on the rear fuselage either side of the roundel, the forward marking the coloured bars of No. 8 Squadron and the rear marking the black and white chequers of No. 43 Squadron the "Fighting Cocks".

Avro Shackleton AEW 2 airplanes in addition to "fighter type" bars also carried the "last two" of the airplanes serial on the fins, and latterly for a time individual airplanes were named after characters of the children's television *Magic Roundabout* programme. Boeing E-3D Sentry AEW 1 airplanes in low-viz markings carry "fighter" style bars on the forward fuselage either side of the low-viz roundel with the "sheathed Arabian dagger" on the fin. Quite uniquely for the second time in its history No. 8 Squadrons airplanes carry dual markings again, since the Sentry Training Flight (Squadron) was granted operational squadron status by way of No. 23 Squadron's number-plate, relinquished when its Tornado F.3 fighters were withdrawn as part of the defence cutbacks in 1994.

However, it should be noted that No.8s famous Arabian Dagger appears prominently on the captains, port side of the aircraft. No. 8 are the only RAF squadron to operate dual marked aircraft. (see aircraft markings). Each airplane also bears the name of one of Disneys "Seven Dwarfs". The two-

Boeing E-3D Sentry AEW

No. 23 (STS) Squadron   RAF Waddington, Lincs,

Boeing E-3D Sentry   (pooled - shared with No. 8 Squadron)

Motto : *Semper aggresus* - Always having attacked

No. 23 Squadron was formed at Fort Grange, Gosport, on 1 September 1915 and flew fighter and reconnaissance missions over the Western Front with F. E. 2bs, Spads, and Sopwith Dolphins before disbanding in December, 1919. On 1 July 1925, No. 23 Squadron reformed at RAF Henlow, Beds, as a fighter unit with Sopwith Snipe, these being successively replaced by Gloster Gamecocks, Bristol Bulldogs, and Hawker Demons before 1938, when it became a twin-engined Bristol Blenheim IF fighter unit. The first part of WW II was taken up with convoy patrol duties, but in 1940, the squadron converted to night fighter operations, subsequently receiving locally modified Boston Havocs and later D. H. Mosquitos, moving to Malta in December 1943, to continue with on air defence and intruder operations until the wars end.

Reformed after the war in 1946, at RAF Wittering, Hunts, No. 23 Squadron continued in the night fighter role with D. H. Vampires, Venoms and Gloster Javelins. It moved to RAF Leuchars, Scotland, in 1963, to receive EE Lightnings relinquishing these in late 1975, for MDC FGR 2 Phantom IIs at the same time moving south to RAF Wattisham, Suffolk. In the spring of 1983, the squadron took up permanent residence in the South Atlantic at RAF Mount Pleasant, until supplanted by No. 1435 Flight whereupon it reformed at RAF Leeming, Yorks, in November 1988, on Panavia Tornado F.3 until 26 February 1994, when the unit was disbanded as part of the defence cutbacks. However, on 1 April 1996, the Air Ministry announced that the E-3A (AEW 1) Sentry Training Flight at the School of Air Warfare, at RAF Waddington, Lincs, should carry the No.23 Squadron banner. The squadrons markings are displayed on the starboard side of the aircraft (No. 8s on the port).

Aircraft markings and codes

The French Spad S 7s were the first No. 23 Squadron airplanes to carry unit markings in the form of a white triangle aft of the fuselage roundel. Following re-equipment with Sopwith Dolphn in March 1918, a white circle was used. Individual aircraft letters were also painted on both types.

Soon after re-formation in 1925, the official 'fighter-type' markings of alternate red and blue squares appeared on Sopwith Snipe, painted along the fuselage sides and across the upper mainplane of the Gloster Gamecocks, Bristol Bulldogs and Hawker Demons that followed. Demons also carried a stylized 'eagle' emblem on the fin, but this was deleted on "Turret Demons" and, following the Munich Crisis, the airplanes were camouflaged and the official code MS- was applied in light-blue forward of the fuselage roundel and an individual airplane letter aft. Bristol Blenheim 1F also carried the MS- code until it changed to YP- in November 1939. A change to night-fighter operations saw the markings 'dumbed down', painted in dull red on Boston Havocs and D. H. Mosquito airplanes, retained post-war until 1951, when the alternate red/blue squares were applied on the booms of the D. H. Vampires and Venom night fighters that followed.

Gloster Javelin all-weather night fighters were unusual in having the squadron markings above the airplanes serial on the engine air intakes. They also carried the 'eagle' emblem on the fin at first without background, but on FAW 7 variants the eagle appeared on a white disc and the intake markings were edged in white. FAW 9 variants appeared minus the red-blue markings, and the eagle was replaced by an individual identification letter on the fin. EE Lightnings saw the appearance of the red/blue squares each side of the nose roundel, and the fuselage spine and fin were painted white, with a the 'eagle' emblem displayed in squadron colours on the white fin. On MDC Phantom IIs, the markings were reversed, a red eagle outlined in white being painted on the nose while the red/blue squares were on the upper fin between horizontal white stripes.

The introduction of low-viz markings saw all markings 'toned down' considerably, the eagle re-appearing in white-edged dull red on the fin. On reformation in the South Atlantic in 1983, a miniature Falkland Islands badge, white on blue background, was appointed on the nose of the Phantoms, flanked by the squadron's red/blue squares. Currently (2002) on the dual marked Boeing E-3D Sentry airplanes a toned down eagle preying on a falcon appears in squadron colours on the starboard side of the fin.

Decorative NATO AWACS Boeing

No. 10 Squadron

RAF Brize Norton, Oxon.   Strategic Transport/Tankers
BAC VC 10 C1K   (10)
Motto : *Rem acu tangere*   'To hit the mark'
Nickname : "Shiny Ten"

No. 10 Squadron formed on 1 January, 1915, for Corps reconnaissance duties in France and as such saw extensive service in WW I equipped with B. E. 2c and F. K . 8. Conversion to the bombing role between the wars saw the squadron flying a succession of Handley Page types including the Hyderabad, Hinaidi and Heyford but by the start of WW II these had been supplanted by A. W. Whitley, which it retained using successive marks until re-equipping with H. P. Halifax in December 1941. Post-war No. 10 Squadron became a transport unit with Douglas Dakota until reverting to bombing again in early 1953, with EE Canberra B. 2 just five years later receiving another Handley Page bomber, the crescent-winged Victor until disbanding in March,1964. On the 1 July 1966, the squadron reformed at RAF Brize Norton with BAC VC 10 C. 1 as a long-range strategic transport unit, beginning scheduled operations in April, 1967. More than three decades later, No.10 still operates its VC.10s from Brize Norton, the squadrons aircraft transporting VIPs, VVIPs, Royalty, Government Ministers, and top military "brass" around the world. However, following conversion of one of the squadrons aircraft for the air-tanking role on 19 June, 1994, No.10 Squadron carried out its first air-to-air refuelling "trail". In 1994, the role change saw the aircraft redesignated VC-10 C.1(K), the "K" denoting "tanker" the squadrons intended primary operational role, now in support of its sister squadron (No.101) also based at Brize Norton with its dedicated VC-10 K tankers.

On the 25 August 1995, the squadron made the last of its twice weekly VC.10 flights to Washington-Dulles in the United States from Brize Norton, a task it had undertaken almost continuously for some twenty five years, excepting for periods in the Falklands Conflict and Gulf War. Also in 1995, No.10 Squadron flew ten sorties to Croatia in support of the NATO Implementation Force in Bosnia, carrying some 1,600 personnel. Having continued to supply tanker aircraft in support of the Bosnia and NATO KFOR operations, in 1999/2000, No.10 Squadron had two tankers on station at Incirlik AB Turkey, and one in the Persian Gulf.

It is intended the original fleet of ten 'white' VC 10s should be progressively withdrawn from use, with one withdrawn and placed in store in April 2001, and another by April 2002.

Long-range
VC10 jet
transport

Aircraft Markings and Codes

Markings on No. 10 Squadron airplanes were introduced in 1916, a disc on the fuselage sides aft of the roundel. A white disc on clear doped BE 2cs and a black on Khaki drab machines. RE 8s initially received similar markings although later a white horizontal bar along the lower fuselage longerons were used.

In March 1918, all squadron markings were removed and not re-applied until the squadron reformed with Dark Green (Nivo) camouflaged Hyderabads in January 1928, which had individual airplane letters in white on each side of the nose and a "winged arrow" badge on the nose and tail. Similar markings were used on H.P. Hinaidis and Vickers Virginia, although H. P. Heyfords had the airplane codes repeated on the fuselage aft of the roundel, and the unit badge on both sides of the nose with Flight colours on the wheel spats.

Unofficial Badge

No. 10 Sqdn.

The squadron's A.W. Whitleys initially carried a large white "10" forward of the fuselage roundel with the individual aircraft letter to the rear. In 1939, the "10" was replaced by the official unit code PB-, later changed to ZA-. Used later on Douglas C-47 Dakota transport planes. But in the Berlin Airlift Operation *Plainfare* all markings except the airplanes letter were removed.

The EE Canberra light-bombers were completely free of markings except for the red "Scampton Wing" speedbird on the nose, changed later on the squadron relocating to RAF Honington, Suffolk, to the "Honington Wing" pheasant in white on the tail. No. 10 Squadron's Canberras detached to Cyprus for the Suez crisis had their serials enlarged and a "winged arrow" appeared in red on the tip-tanks. Yellow and black stripes were painted around the fuselage and across the wings. H. P. Victor B. Is carried no individual markings except a squadron badge on the nose just forward of the entrance door and a representation of the "winged arrow" on the fin above the (RAF) stripes.

The squadron's BAC VC 10s were initially free of individual markings, however on Armistice Day 1968, each of the squadron's airplanes were allocated an RAF VCs name to be painted on the forward fuselage cockpit area. Also above the royal-blue transport "cheat line" in black lettering over the years has appeared, in succession, RAF Transport Command, RAF Air Support Command, RAF Support Command and now just Royal Air Force. Also a squadron badge on the nose and the airplanes "Last Three" appears on the fin.

No. 10 Squadron BAC VC 10 C. 1 transport   (RAF)

No. 10 Squadron VC 10 C. 1K tanker/transport dispensing fuel to four   (RAF)
Sepecat Jaguar strike planes

Tactical Transport   (Lockheed C-130 Hercules)

No. 24 Squadron

RAF Lyneham, Wilts. Lyneham Tactical Airlift Wing
Lockheed Hercules C1/ C3/C 4/C5 (44 aircraft pooled)
Motto : *In omnia parati* - 'Prepared for all things'

Formed on 1 September 1915, at Hounslow Heath, No. 24 Squadron was one of the RAF's early scout units and went to France with Airco D. H. 2 airplanes. It was later equipped with improved Airco D. H. 5s and then the superb S.E. 5A before disbanding on 1 February, 1920, having recorded some 300 "kills". Re-established two months later at Kenley, it became a communications and VIP transport squadron a role it retained throughout WW II. The squadron used a variety of types until standardising on type with the Avro York used in the Berlin airlift the airplanes crewed by personnel from all over the Commonwealth. In addition post-war between June 1946 and December 1949, the squadron operated the Avro Lancastrian C.2 transport developed specifically for the RAF post-war from the wartime Avro Lancaster bomber. The squadron has remained on transport duties ever since. It was the first to equip with the Handley Page Hastings at RAF Bassingbourn in December, 1950 and flew the type until January 1968, when it moved to RAF Colerne near Bath, in the west of England to receive the ubiquitous Lockheed Hercules C-130 tactical transport. Variously operating the C. 1, C.1K, C. 3 and C.3P variants today the squadron operates the greatly improved C-130J/30 recently introduced into RAF service designated C4 and C.5 for the stretched variant respectively.

Since moving to RAF Lyneham, in February 1968, the squadron was designated a tactical transport unit, subsequently flying many special operations around the world, including rescue missions, disaster relief, refugee evacuation, and garrison support missions, as well as famine relief drops in Nepal, Ethiopia and Sudan. In November 1975, the squadron relinquished its airborne assault role, with the greater portion of its tasks, involving strategic transport duties on scheduled routes, although tactical support tasks still remained a primary role. During the Falklands War, No.24 was heavily involved in maintaining the bridgehead between the UK and Ascension Island. It is now more than thirty years since the unit re-equipped with the venerable "Herky Bird" (Fat Albert) as part of the four squadron Transport Wing at RAF Lyneham, a role in which it seems set to continue for many years to come. Since operating the Hercules no squadron markings have been carried as the aircraft are drawn from the Lyneham Central Servicing Wing as required.

Lockheed Hercules 25 years in RAF service celebration livery

No. 30 Squadron

RAF Lyneham, Wilts. Lyneham Tactical Airlift Wing
Lockheed Hercules C 4/C5 (aircraft pooled)
Motto : *Ventre a terre* — 'All out'

No. 30 Squadron formed at Farnborough in 1914, and was immediately dispatched to Mesopotamia to fly against the Turks throughout WW I with a miscellany of airplanes. Post-WW I it went to Baghdad flying RAF R. E. 8s and later Airco D. H. 9 day bombers, Westland Wapitis and Hawker Hardys for policing duties, entering WW II with Bristol Blenheims which it used in the Western Desert. The squadron took part in the Greece and Crete operations before returning to Egypt to re-equip with Hawker Hurricane fighters. It later moved to Ceylon and Burma to join SEAC in the war against the Japanese, converting to Thunderbolts in July 1944. Hawker Tempest were used until December 1946, when the squadron disbanded, reforming in 1947, with Douglas Dakota C 4 transports. Later Vickers Valetta were received and in 1957, the lumbering Blackburn Beverley which the squadron operated in Kenya and Bahrain in 1964. This author experiencing one of the most horrendous flights of his life whilst flying in one of the squadrons airplanes at this time from RAF Muharraq to Sharjah, when, having encountered severe turbulence the Beverley would suddenly drop like a 'brick' several tens of feet and on climbing back to altitude would repeat the whole unpleasant experience over again.

The run down of RAF Middle East Command, saw the squadron cease operations on 6 September 1967, and on return to the UK No.30 Squadron disbanded. Reformation was inaugurated on 1 May 1968 at RAF Fairford, Gloucestershire, with its first Lockheed Hercules C.1s arriving on the 10 June 1968. The squadron joined Air Support Command, for route flying and tactical transport duties. Concentration of Hercules assets at RAF Lyneham, saw the squadron relocate to the Wiltshire base during February 1971, from where it still operates today as part of the Tactical Transport Wing. The squadron played a major part in the Falklands Campaign, Operation *Corporate* in 1982, later flying C1K "tankers" on detachment, supporting the UK - Falklands Air Bridge, until the four aircraft detachment at Port Stanley Airport was redesignated No.1312 Flight on 20 August 1983. Recent re-equipment with the C-130J variant determines the squadron will remain part of the Tactical Transport fleet for many years to come, although whether at RAF Lyneham remains to be seen as a move to Brize Norton has been muted. Currently in line with 'pooling' of airplanes at Lyneham no squadron markings are carried on the C 4s or C 5s. No Squadron markings are carried.

Unofficial Badge

No. 47 Squadron

RAF Lyneham, Wilts. Lyneham Tactical Airlift Wing
Lockheed Hercules C 4/C5 (aircraft pooled)
Motto : *Nili nomen roboris omen*
'The name of the Nile is an omen of our strength'

Formed in 1 March, 1916, at Beverley, Yorks, for the Home Defence of Hull No. 47 Squadron started flying in Macedonia against the Bulgarians in WW I, and immediately post-war it served in South Russia against the Bolsheviks. Between the wars it was retained in the battle order for policing work in the Sudan. In WW II initially the unit flew Bristol Beauforts and Beaufighters in the anti-shipping role in the Mediterranean and in 1944 in Burma where it re-equipped with D. H. Mosquitos. Post-war the squadron reformed in the UK with Handley Page Halifax transports for operations with the airborne forces until taking part in the Berlin Airlift with H. P. Hastings. These were replaced by Blackburn Beverleys in 1956 until disbanding on 31 October 1967. However, it was not long until the unit resumed transport duties again when it reformed at RAF Fairford, Glous, on 25 February 1968, with Lockheed Hercules C.1, C.2 transports procured from the U.S. by the Wilson Labour Government in the early 1960s. On 1 February 1971, No.47 Squadron relocated to RAF Lyneham, Wilts, where it remains to this day as part of the Lyneham Transport Wing. The unit is one of the two Hercules squadrons trained on tactical support and Special Forces duties, and its skills were to put use during Operation *Corporate* the recapture of the Falkland Islands.

On 29 December 1993, a Hercules of No.47 Squadron flew the 1,000th humanitarian relief mission into Sarajavo, bringing the total load carried to nearly 15,000 tonnes (more than carried during the Berlin Airlift of the early 1950s). An RAF Hercules aircraft flew an average of three sorties a day from Ancona in Italy, each airlift conveying some 15 tonnes. Currently the squadrons future appears secure as it commences operation of the new Lockheed Hercules C-130J airplane (RAF C.4, C.5) which has just entered service with the RAF and is in essence an entirely "new" transport airplane. It was decided to procure 25 Lockheed Hercules C-130J aircraft to replace ageing earlier C-130 Hercules transports. Currently it is proposed that Britain should participate in the Airbus, FLA project, with a view to later replacing further life-expired C-130 Hercules with this airplane. The C-130J-30 (long-fuselage) type is designated Hercules C. Mk.4 (15) and C.Mk.5 (10) (C-130J) respectively in RAF service. No squadron markings are carried

Unofficial Badge

No. 57(R) Squadron

RAF Lyneham, Wilts. Tactical Airlift Wing Hercules OCU
Lockheed Hercules C1/C3 and C4/C5 Conversion Flight (5)
Motto : *Corpus non animum muto* 'The body changes not the spirit'

Unofficial Badge

No. 57 Squadron formed on 8 June, 1916, at Copmanthorpe for high-altitude reconnaissance. On moving to France on 16 December 1916, with F. E. 2d for fighter-recce duties, in May 1917 it received Airco D. H. 4s for day bombing, until disbanding on 31 December 1919. The squadron reformed as a bomber unit on 5 September 1932, successively operating Hawker Harts and Hinds, until receiving Bristol Blenheim Is in March 1938, before receiving heavy night bombers by way of the Vickers Wellington and Avro Lancaster for the bombing offensive against Germany in WW II. Post-WW II the squadron remained in the bomber role with Avro Lincoln, the interim Boeing B-29 Washington until receiving EE Canberra B. 2 until it became part of the V-force with Handley Page Victors in March 1959. Latterly the squadron operated the Victor in the in-flight refuelling role with its Victor K 1A/K.2 tankers, taking part in the renowned Avro Vulcan bombing run to the South Atlantic in 1982, when no less than sixteen Victor tankers were needed to get the bomber there and back. No. 57 Squadrons Victor tankers were flown from Marham until 30 June 1986, when the squadron disbanded as Lockheed Tristar and H.S. VC 10 tankers began to enter RAF service. The squadron was resurrected on 1 July 1992, as No.57 (Reserve) Squadron at RAF Lyneham, Wilts, when No. 242 Hercules OCU was granted Reserve squadron status, a role in which the squadron continues until this day, with new responsibilities for conversion training on the new C-130J Hercules which is virtually a new aeroplane with an all electronic cockpit with a two man crew. Easily distinguishable on the tarmac by its six-bladed propellers as opposed to the four-bladed assemblies used on the C-130s. No squadron markings are carried.

Lockheed Hercules C4/ C5 (C-130J/30) now partially equip the RAF's Tactical Airlift Wing

No. 70 Squadron   RAF Lyneham, Wilts, Tactical Airlift Wing
Lockheed Hercules C1P/C3P (shared with No. 24 Squadron)
Motto: *Usquam* — 'Anywhere'

Unofficial Badge

No. 70 Squadron formed at Farnborough in 1916, and went to France with Sopwith 1½ Strutters. It became the first RFC squadron to have a synchronised machine gun firing forward through the propeller arc, as standard fitted to its airplanes. Later as a highly successful scout unit the squadron flew Sopwith Camels on fighter patrols and ground attack duties until the Armistice. In 1920, following a short period of disbandment the squadron reformed with Vickers Vimys, and saw service in Egypt, later operating Vickers Vernon, Victorias and Valentias in Iraq in the bomber-transport role. During WW II the squadron flew Vickers Wellington bombers in the Mediterranean, Italy and the Western Desert. Post-war the squadron remained in the Middle East with Avro Lancasters as its standard equipment until returning to the transport role, initially with Douglas Dakota,Vickers Valetta, H. P. Hastings and a mixture of A. W. Argosies and Lockheed Hercules before returning to the UK at RAF Lyneham, Wilts, in January, 1975.

Since returning to Lyneham the squadron has continued with its routine operations and relief work as required and it took an active part in Operation *Corporate* in 1982, in support of recovery of the Falkland Islands, gaining the distinction of making the longest Hercules flight to date, when on 18 June 1982, a No. 70 Squadron crew from Ascension Island, flew to East Falklands and back non-stop, making a night supply drop of Rapier missile battery spares, the air refuelled sortie taking 28 hours and 4 minutes. Today, the squadron remains at Lyneham, where it continues to operate its Lockheed Hercules aircraft. As with the other squadrons operating 'pooled' airplanes, no squadron markings are displayed.

Lockheed Hercules C 3P receives attention on the flight-line

No. 32 (Royal) Squadron

RAF Northolt (London) Comms/ VIP, VVIP transport
BAe 146 CC2 (2), HS/BAe 125 CC3 (5)
Eurocopter Twin Squirrel HCC 1 (3) VIP
Air Hanson, Sikorsky S-76C plus (1) VVIP
Motto : *Adeste comites* - 'Rally round comrades'

No. 32

No. 32 Squadron was traditionally a fighter squadron having been formed at Netheravon in January 1916, for service in France with Airco D. H. 2s, D. H. 5s and RAF S. E. 5As before the end of the war. Between the wars it was one of the Biggin Hill squadrons successively operating Sopwith Snipe, Gloster Grebe, Gloster Gamecock, A. W. Siskin, Bristol Bulldog and Gloster Gauntlet biplane fighters, before receiving Hawker Hurricane monoplanes with which it fought in the Battle of Britain. In 1942, it moved to North Africa and the Mediterranean remaining there until 1969, with D. H. Vampire and Venom fighter-bombers before changing roles to bombing and receiving EE Canberras in March, 1957 until disbanding in 1969, to take over the duties of the Metropolitan Communications Squadron (MCS) at RAF Northolt. The MCS assumed the No. 32 Squadron mantle, and during 1992 it absorbed the duties of No. 60 Squadron, a comms unit, formerly based at Wildenrath, Germany when that squadron was withdrawn. On the 31 March, 1995, the squadron absorbed the Queens Flight, to gain its unique title, again restructured into three flights, with its complement of, H.S.125 CC.2 (2), BAe 125 CC.3 (6), Gazelle HCC.4 (4) BAe 146 CC.2 (3) and two Westland Wessex HCC.4 (2). During the Gulf War No. 32 Squadron contributed one of its BAe 125 CC. 3 for in-theatre communications duties.

Since 1996, a number of inventory changes have occurred, cost cutting exercises, forcing a reduction in aircraft and types on strength with a degree of civilianisation creeping in. On the 1 April 1996, two civilian Aerospatiale AS.355F1 Twin Squirrel helicopters with military registrations (ZJ139 and ZJ 140) replaced the Gazelles for use as VIP transports. The H.S./BAE 125 fleet has been reduced to just four civilian operated (RAF crewed) airplanes and the two aged Wessex HCC.4 helicopters after twenty nine years service, have been replaced by a single Air Hanson Sikorsky S-76C Plus aircraft. Currently there is a possibility that an Airbus Industries passenger airliner (A320 - of which there are plenty on the second-hand market) may be added to the fleet as a USAF style "Air Force One" although at the present time this is still open to speculation but with the withdrawal of BAe 146-100 serial ZE702 in December 2001, likely to become reality, soon.

Sadly before concluding this brief recount of No.32 Squadrons proud history, it must be told that on the 31 August 1997, the squadron was called upon to deploy one of its resplendent BAe 146 airplane to Charles de Gaulle Airport, Paris, to carry out the sombre task of returning the body of Diana, Princess of Wales to Britain for her funeral and eventual incarceration at her ancestral home at Althorp, Northamptonshire, following the fatal car accident in Paris that year.

Aircraft Markings and Codes

No squadron markings are carried on No. 32 Squadrons airplanes but the various types have their own distinctive livery. The Air Hanson VVIP S 76C Plus civil registration G-XXEA is finished in an overall maroon colour scheme similar to that applied to the original Airspeed AS.6J Envoy III specially fitted out for the Kings Flight in 1936, with the original registration G-AEXX reversed. As detailed.

The surviving HS/BAe 125 communications airplanes are in low-viz European grey with low-viz national markings applied. The two BAe 146 CC 2s are in distinctive red/white livery with a blue flash along the middle of the fuselage and a red tail. The two leased Aerospatiale AS 355F1 Twin Squirrel HCC 1s operated by Operational Support Services a division of McAlpine Helicopters appear in that companies livery with military registrations.

G-XXEA—Now—VVIP Sikorsky S76C Plus

G-AEXX—Then (1936) Airspeed Envoy—in same livery

(RAF)

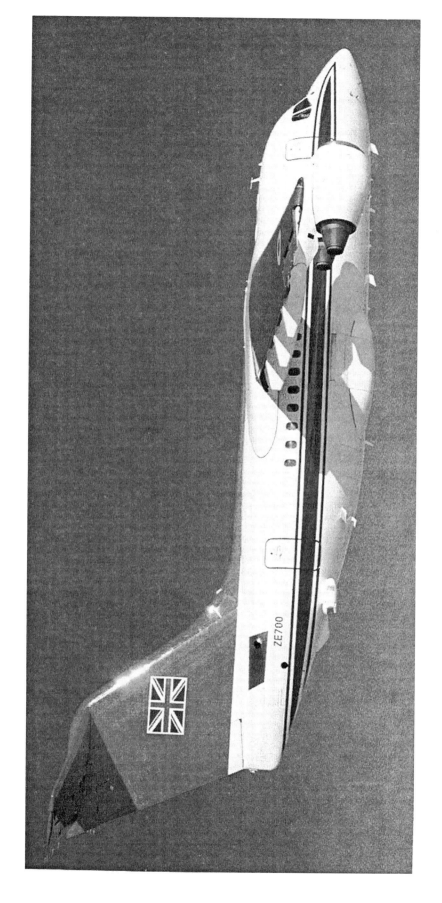

No 32 Squadron VIP transport one of two BAe 146-100 airplanes on inventory (ZE700, ZE701)

(RAF)

No. 39 (1 PRU) Squadron   RAF Marham, Norfolk,   Strategic Reconnaissance/Survey
EE Canberra PR 9 (4), T. 4 (1)
Motto: *Die noctuque* - 'By day and night'

Unofficial Badge

No. 39 Squadron formed at Hounslow in April, 1915, as the first anti-Zeppelin Home Defence unit of the RFC equipped with B. E. 2c. Re-equipped as a fighter unit with Bristol Fighters and F. E. 2bs before the cessation of hostilities. Between the wars initially the squadron re-equipped with D. H. 9A day-bombers at Risalpur in India (now part of Pakistan) with the Westland Wapiti before receiving Hawker Hart which it retained until the outbreak of WW II. During WW II the squadron operated mainly in the Middle East with Bristol Blenheim, Beaufort, Beaufighter and American Martin Marauder IIIs. Post-war No.39 Squadron returned briefly to Africa, then served in Egypt and Malta, with D. H. Mosquitos, Hawker Tempest, and Gloster Meteor NF 11/13 night fighters until it received the first of the EE Canberra PR 3 photo reconnaissance variants. Returning to the UK it remained in the photo recce role until 1982, when it was downgraded to Flight status as No. 1 PRU (Photographic Reconnaissance Unit), a title it retained on reforming as No. 39 (1 PRU) Squadron again on 1 July, 1992.

It was reported in 2000 that a replacement for the squadrons thirty-five year old airplanes is still under consideration. Favourite is the latest variant of the American Lockheed U.2 high altitude "Spy Plane", although currently it is intended to keep the Canberra in service until 2009. Recent operational duties which have included a number of aerial surveys for various overseas countries was the deployment to Afghanistan for high-altitude reconnaissance duties in the war against terrorism.

Current squadron airplanes are hemp coloured and unit markings include the squadron badge on the tail-fin, a winged bomb on a light-blue disc. Aircraft two-letter identifications are prefixed 'A' for No. 39 Squadron.

No. 39 (1 PRU) Squadron EE Canberra PR9 shows clearly 'fighter-style' offset cockpit configuration   (RAF)

The forward nose section of the PR 9 hinges open to permit the navigator entry to the airplane. His only contact with the outside world once in situ is via the small rectangular panel seen immediately above the ejection seat symbols

No. 39

The Canberra PR 9 navigator in situ

Not quite ready—a last look at the flight plan before the feet are drawn inside

No. 51 Squadron   RAF Waddington, Lincs.   Electronic Surveillance (ELINT/SIGINT)
                          HS Nimrod R.. 1P (E.1) (3)
                          Motto : 'Swift and Sure'

No. 51 Squadron formed on 15 May, 1916, at Thetford, Norfolk, for Home Defence a role in which the squadron served throughout WW I until disbanding on 13 June, 1919. Reformed in 1937, initial equipment comprised Avro Anson and Vickers Virginias until it transferred to A. W. Whitleys in February 1938, with successive marks flown until re-equipping with H. P. Halifax bombers in November 1942. These flown throughout the war, until the unit assumed the transport role in 1946, with Short Stirling V and Avro Yorks flown on the Berlin Airlift before being disbanded on 31 October 1950. The present squadron formed on 21 August, 1958, when the then ELINT No. 192 Squadron equipped with specially modified Canberras and D. H. Comet C.2R for electronic reconnaissance missions was re-numbered No. 51 Squadron. The Comets were replaced by specially modified Nimrod R.1 in 1974. HS Nimrod R.1s had been originally selected for the task, as far back as July 1971. Following disposal of the remaining Canberras in the late 1970s, the Nimrod R.1s acquired in 1974, became solely responsible for carrying out the units tasks under the auspices of No.18 Group, Strike Command. In August 1990, a 28-man crew of a No. 51 Squadron Nimrod R.1 based at RAF Wyton claimed a world record by reaching a cumulative crew total of 266,569 mission hours in the air. In the same month the squadrons three reconnaissance aircraft were deployed to RAF Akrotiri, Cyprus, as part of Operation *Granby* build up in the Gulf.

Since 1995, the squadron has been heavily involved in SIGINT, COMINT and ELINT gathering missions, monitoring radio, telephone and other communications particularly over the former Yugoslavia and more recently (2002) in Afghanistan. Following an unfortunate ditching accident near their base at RAF Kinloss, Scotland, on 16 May 1995, one of the units three special missions aircraft was replaced by a Nimrod MR 2 (XV249) modified to R1.P standard by BAE Systems at their Avro Woodford facility. Having returned to full strength and a with a move to RAF Waddington, Air Warfare Centre in 1996, No.51 Squadron appears set to continue in its designated Special Duties role with its updated BAe Nimrod R.1Ps for many years to come. Current hemp coloured airplanes carry a red goose in flight, from the squadrons badge, on the tail at the base of the fin. The two-numeral airplane identification is also displayed in white on the fin.

No 51 Squadron R. 1 HS Nimrod

No. 99 Squadron

RAF Brize Norton, Oxon. Strategic Transport/Heavy Lift
Boeing/MDC C-17A Globemaster III (4)
Motto : *Quisque tenax* - (Each tenacious)

No. 99 Squadron formed on 15 August, 1917, at Yatesbury, Wilts, with D.H.6 and B.E.2c. In March 1918, the squadron received 18 Airco D.H.9 day bombers with which it moved to France in April 1918, as a day bomber squadron, joining Trenchards, Independent Force. During just six months of operational service in WW I the squadron made 76 raids and dropped a total of 61 tons of bombs. Of all the squadrons aircraft that set out on raids, 79% succeeded in reaching and bombing their targets, a not inconsiderable feat when considering the distances flown mostly over hostile enemy territory and the concerted opposition put up against these daylight raids - not to mention the unreliability at the time of the D.H.9s Puma engines. In September 1918, the squadron re-equipped with the much improved Airco D.H.9A. In May 1919, it left for India, where it was subsequently engaged in the Mahsud and Waziristan operations on the North-West Frontier, until, on 1 April 1920, it was renumbered No.27 Squadron.

On 1 April 1924, No. 99 Squadron reformed at Netheravon, then in August 1924, it became the only unit to receive the Avro Aldershot heavy night bomber. In December 1925, it became the first RAF squadron to receive H. P. Hyderabads at Bircham Newton which supplanted the Aldershots. October 1929, saw the start of deliveries of the Hyderabads development, the Hinaidi. Again No. 99 Squadron was the first to receive the type. Then in November 1933, it became the first unit to receive H.P. Heyfords flown until October 1938.

In October 1938, conversion to Vickers Wellington began, and later at RAF Mildenhall, Suffolk, the squadron started flying leaflet drops over Germany. Leaflet-drops continued until the German's invasion of Norway in April 1940, when anti-shipping operations began with the bombing of the *Tirpitz* in January 1941, the *Gneisenau* and *Scharnhorst* along with raids on the Ruhr and Berlin. On 14 January 1942, squadron operations in the UK ceased and the unit left for India and night bombing raids began on Japanese bases in Burma in November 1942. Having operated successive marks of Wellingtons, in September 1944, the squadron converted to Consolidated Liberators for long-range bombing attacks and in June 1945, it moved to the Cocos Islands in preparation for the invasion of Malaya. Some flights involving sorties of sixteen or more hours duration, with particular attention paid to the notorious Siam-Burma railway. After flying some anti-shipping strikes with the Liberators the squadron disbanded on 15 November 1945 in the Cocos Islands.

Two days later at RAF Lyneham, in the UK, No. 99 Squadron reformed with Avro York C.1 transports, re-equipping with H. P. Hastings transports in August 1949. During the Suez Crisis, No. 99 operated from Cyprus dropping troops in the Port Said area. June 1959, saw the arrival of the first Bristol Britannia C.1, C.2 turbo-prop transports which were operated by Transport Command and its successor Air Support Command world-wide until the squadron finally disbanded on 6 January 1976 at RAF Brize Norton. No. 99 Squadron reformed at Brize Norton again a quarter of a century later receiving its first Globemaster III on 17 May, 2001. The four long-range strategic transports give the RAF many new capabilities, although some criticism has been made of the strict terms of the seven-year lease of the airplanes,not allowing the RAF to use the airplane's formidable tactical and airdrop capabilities, with penalties imposed for exceeding the agreed number of annual flying hours. Nevertheless No. 99 Squadron has already received its 'baptism of fire' having been called on to support UK operations in Afghanistan in the war against terrorism in 2002.

In RAF service the airplanes retain their drab grey colour scheme as used by the USAF Air Mobility Command, with the squadrons leaping black Puma displayed on the tail-fin outlined in red. Royal Air Force in black appears on the forward fuselage with a miniaturized Union Jack immediately above the freight compartment door.

No. 99 Squadron unofficial
badge circa 1920/30s

USAF AMC Globemaster III in similar light-grey finish to RAF airplane

104.

Reformed No. 99 Squadron Boeing Globemaster III (note tail-fin marking)

No. 101 Squadron

RAF Brize Norton, Oxon, In-flight refuelling
BAC VC 10 K3/K4   (8)
Motto : *Mena agitat molem* - 'Mind over matter'

Unofficial Badge

First formed in July 1917, No. 101 Squadron was initially engaged on night bombing duties and operated the F. E. 2 in France on the Western Front until its return to England and subsequent disbandment in 1919. After reforming in March 1928, it later became the only operational RAF unit to use the Boulton and Paul Sidestrand medium day bomber which it flew from 1929 until 1935 when these were replaced by the Overstrand. At the start of WW II No. 101 Squadron was equipped with Bristol Blenheim until 1941, when the Vickers Wellington heavy bomber were taken on charge. Although these were soon replaced by the ubiquitous Avro Lancaster which were used extensively by the squadron on night bombing raids on Germany. Unfortunately No. 101 Squadron has the rather dubious WW II record of sustaining more casualties than any other squadron. Post-war the squadron re-equipped with Avro Lincoln which it operated until 1951, when it became the first squadron to received EE Canberra jet bombers with which it deployed to Malaya where it undertook offensive operations against the communist terrorists. Disbanded in February 1957, it was soon reinstated in the battle order, this time with Avro Vulcan B.1 at RAF Finningley, Yorks in January 1958. A move to RAF Waddington followed in June 1961, where No 101 received the B. 2 variant during 1967, becoming operational January 1968. Disbanded as part of the Vulcan bomber phase-out in 1982, No. 101 Squadron officially reformed on 1 May 1984 at RAF Brize Norton with BAC VC 10 tankers for in-flight refuelling duties. On the 1 May 1984, at RAF Brize Norton as a flight refuelling unit receiving its first BAC VC 10 tanker on 27 September 1985. Subsequently the squadron has received and operates the dedicated K 2, K 3 and K 4 tanker variants having been heavily involved in the defence of the UK, the Gulf War, and the Balkan conflicts as an invaluable force multiplier not only to the RAF but numerous Allied air forces including the United States. More recent operations have involved the squadron in coalition forces operations in Afghanistan. Currently the squadrons airplanes are hemp coloured and carry a red lion behind a yellow castle turret on a small black disc no the fin, with a large individual airplane identification letter in white above it.

The new Eurofighter re-
ceives a 'top-up'

106.

No. 101 Squadron 'Flying the Flag'

No. 101 Squadron with its GR 1 Tornado's Nellis AFB, Nevada April 1997 the
airplanes guest's at the USAF's 50th Anniversary celebrations

No. 101 Squadron 'hemp' coloured VC 10 K tanker awaits another in-flight refuelling mission

No. 101 Squadron VC refuelling two Sepecat Jaguars

108.

No. 216 Squadron

RAF Brize Norton, Oxon. Strategic Transport and air refuelling
Lockheed Tristar K 1, KC1, C2, C2A (8)
Motto: *CCXVI dona ferens* - '216 bearing gifts'

Unofficial Badge

No. 216 Squadron formed on 1 April, 1918, from No. 16 Squadron RNAS at Villesneux with Handley Page O/400s with Trenchards Independent Force. Post-WW I it redeployed to Egypt using six O/400s on mail and passenger transport duties, a role it has retained ever since. In the 1930s the squadron operated Bristol Bombay bomber-transports then Douglas C-47 Dakota in WW II. Based in the Middle East until the 1950s in 1956 the squadron returned to Lyneham to receive D. H. Comet C. 2 then the world's first military jet transport. It later operated the improved C. 4 version until it disbanded in 1975. The squadron was briefly resurrected in 1979, to fly Blackburn Buccaneer strike-bombers, but was disbanded again within the year when the airplanes were grounded with wing fatigue problems. Subsequently in 1984, the squadron reformed to operate the six Lockheed Tristar fleet that were crewed initially in RAF service by their former owners British Airways. Later when three further airplanes were purchased from Pan AM, some were converted to dual tanker/transports by Marshall Aerospace of Cambridge. On 12 May 1995, No.216 Squadron passed ten years of flying its Tristar aircraft to and from the South Atlantic in support of the Falkland Islands garrison. The journey via the USAF staging base on Ascension Island, had by that time been successfully completed more than 1,100 times since their commencement in the late Spring of 1985. Currently, 2002, No.216 operates a mix of nine Tristar aircraft comprising K.1, KC.1, and (series 500) C.2, C.2A aircraft, from its Oxfordshire base. Having throughout 1999/2000, based one aircraft at Ancona, Italy, in support of No.4 Squadron's BAe Harrier GR 7 operations at Gioia del Colle, air base Italy. Operation *Engadine*.

Currently the squadron's livery is representative of the old Transport Command colours with an eagle in flight with a bomb in its claws displayed on the fin, standard red, white, and blue roundel and fin stripes with Royal Air Force displayed in black centrally on the fuselage above a black cheat-line.

No 216 Squadron VC 10 K.1 preparing to leave RAF Akrotiri, Cyprus

No 216 Squadron C.1

No 216 Squadron C.2 at Brize Norton prepares for flight

No. 3 Group

Badge :   Three swords in pile, the points upwards, and
     each enfiled by an astral crown
Motto :   *"Niet zonder arbyt"* (Nothing without labour)
Authority :   King George VI, August, 1947.

The three swords in the pile denote the warlike activity of the Group. The three astral crowns are symbolically representative of the three Royal Abesses of Ely, the daughters of the Christian King Anna (A.D. 650) of Exning, who gave his life fighting against the Pagan hordes. No 3 Group's Headquarters were situated near Exning, the old East Anglia capital. (The units of this Group operated from airfields located around Ely. As the Arms of the See of Ely include three crowns, and the number of the Group is three, this number of astral crowns was chosen for the badge.) The old Dutch motto meaning "Nothing without Labour" was taken from the house of Cornelius Vermuyden, a Dutch engineer who reclaimed 40,000 acres of local fen. The Dutch motto was adopted to commemorate the fact that most of the Group's operations took aircraft over Holland on their way to Germany in WW II, and also for the help given to our aircrews who landed in that country.

No. 3 (Bomber) Group was formed on 1 May 1936, with its headquarters at Andover, Hants, moving to RAF Mildenhall, Suffolk, in January, 1937. Moving to Exning, Suffolk, in March 1940, the Group H.Q returned to Mildenhall in January 1947, and on 1 November 1967, merged with No. 1 Group. The Strike Command re-organisation of 1 April 2000, gave rise to a new No. 3 Group headquartered at Northwood, by redesignating No. 18 (Maritime) Group, formed on 28 November, 1969.

Inventory (includes Reserve (R) Squadrons - OCUs) :
HS Nimrod MR. 2   (24) — Nos. 42(R), 120, 201, and 206 Squadrons
Westland Sea King HAR 3 (17) — Nos. 22, 78, 202 Squadrons
Westland Sea King HAR 3A (6) — No. 203(R) Squadron
Harrier GR 7 / Sea Harrier F/A 2 (74) — Nos 1, 3, 4 (RAF) Nos. 800, 801 (FAA) Joint RAF/RN - 2005
Note: It was announced in 2002 that the FAA Sea Harrier F/A 2 would be wfu circa 2006/2007 or the entire fleet and a carrier (Invincible) might be sold to India.

Maritime Patrol.
The only full-time dedicated maritime aircraft in the RAF's 21st Century Battle O
rder are three squadrons of HS/BAE Nimrods. Interestingly the RAF is the only air arm in the world to use an all-jet maritime patrol plane, powered by four R-R RB. 168-20 Spey Mk 250 turbofans each rated at 54.00 kN (12,140-lb) s.t. The Nimrod is a potent ASW (Anti-Submarine Warfare) airplane, in times of war to be used to deny the enemy effective use of his submarines by overt or covert surveillance, and direct attack. The airplane can detect, locate, identify, track and engage an enemy submarine entirely autonomously, or can do so in conjunction with friendly ships, submarines and other land-based or ship-based fixed wing or rotary wing aircraft. Nimrod also has a vital ASV (Anti-Surface Vessel) role, detecting, locating, identifying and shadowing enemy surface vessels and can attack them with long-range missiles. At other times rather than undertake a direct attack against a heavily defended vessel, the Nimrod can 'stand off' and provide information and directions for other ships, helicopters, or other maritime strike/attack planes to undertake their own raids and attacks.

With a total of 46 Nimrod MR Mk 1s delivered since October, 1969, the force has declined dramatically since its Cold War peak with five operational squadrons. It has however, played its part on various operations since and including the Falklands War in important peace-keeping and UN enforcement operations in the Gulf and the Adriatic, as well as supporting search-and-rescue operations and North Sea oil-field protection duties from its base at Kinloss in north-east Scotland.

HS Nimrod MR 1s began to replace the aging Avro Shackleton MR 3 in late 1969, subsequently 35 receiving improved mission system, EMI Searchwater radar, and improved armaments in the late 1970s. Currently (2002), the RAF has 24 MR 2s of which three are in storage. Eighteen of the twenty-four MR 2s are being rebuilt to MRA 4 standard for service well into the 21st Century. Amazingly 80% of the Nimrod's airframe will be dismantled and some 60% will actually be replaced, including the entire wing and centre section. The new wing will contain increased fuel tankage and four new, highly fuel-efficient BMW R-R BR 710 turbofans with their ducts and intakes. As might be expected with an undertaking of this magnitude the project is already two years behind schedule, with service entry of the first modified airplane not expected until 2005. It is of interest the first three airframes earmarked for modification were transported to the sub-contractor at Hurn Airport, Bournemouth, in the south of England, by a Heavylift Soviet-built Antonov An-124 Condor transport plane, after first having their wings and tail-fin removed at the Kinloss base. Subsequently all modification work is being undertaken by the prime contractor (BAE Systems) at his Woodford facility in the north of England.

No 3 Group

HS/BAe Nimrod MR2. The world's only jet-powered maritime patrol plane

No. 42(R) Squadron

RAF Kinloss, Morayshire, Scotland.   No. 236 Nimrod OCU
HS/BAe Nimrod MR. 2 (3)
Motto : *Fortiter in re* - 'Bravely in action'

Formed on the 1 April, 1916, at Filton as a Corps reconnaissance unit No. 42 Squadron went to France, then spent some time in Italy, until returning to France again flying B. E. 2es and R. E. 8s during WW I. Soon after the Armistice the squadron returned to the UK disbanding on 26 June, 1919. Reformed in 1936, it was assigned the torpedo-bomber role with Vickers Vildebeest, later using Bristol Beauforts on shipping strikes off Norway. A move to India followed in 1942, to fly Bristol Blenheims and later Hawker Hurricane fighter-bombers in Burma. At the end of the war it re-equipped with Republic Thunderbolt IIs until disbanding in December, 1945. For a year from October 1946, the squadron operated the Bristol Beaufighter TF X torpedo fighter as the sole strike unit with Coastal Command until disbanding on 15 October, 1947.

On 28 June 1952, No.42 Squadron reformed at St Eval, Cornwall, as a Coastal Command maritime reconnaissance unit, equipped with Avro Shackleton maritime patrol planes from a nucleus provided by No. 220 Squadron. In June 1955, No.42 Squadrons Avro Shackleton MR. 2s with the onset of the EOKA troubles in Cyprus assumed a secondary troop carrying role, which was to be repeated in November 1956, in support of the Suez operations. Earlier in 1956, the Shackleton MR.2 airplanes replaced the Avro Lincolns based in Aden becoming the Colonial Policing Squadron tasked with aerial bombing and photography supporting No 8 (F) Squadron. In 1958, the squadron handed over the Colonial Policing role to other Shackleton units, including Nos.224, 228 and No. 37 Squadron. On 8 October 1958, the squadron returned to the UK to RAF St Mawgan, where many hours were spent on air-sea-rescue standby and patrol, with detachments to Aden and Majunga, Mozambique in 1967, assisting with the Beira Blockade (oil tanker) during the first year of the Rhodesian UDI crisis. Continuing in the maritime reconnaissance role conversion to HS Nimrod M.R.1s commenced in April 1971. Eleven years later in 1982, the squadron went to war again when within 24 hours of receiving the order that two Nimrod MR.2s were dispatched to the Ascension Islands, for the first phase of Operation *Corporate,* the recovery of the Falkland Islands. Sorties were flown deep into the South Atlantic in support of RAF aircraft, Royal Naval ships and submarines in an extremely intense period between April - May 1982, before other Nimrod MR.2s from the Kinloss Wing took over the tasks.

In 1992, No.38 (Reserve) Squadron was redesignated No.42 (Reserve) Squadron NOCU; which today remains at RAF Kinloss, flying Nimrod MR.2s which are currently undergoing upgrade to Nimrod 2000 (MR.4) standard for use well into the next century, although delays and undermanning of the upgrade work means the RAF will not now be flying Nimrod MR.4s until well until the new millenium. Currently no squadron markings are carried as the airplanes are drawn from a central pool.

No. 120 Squadron

RAF Kinloss, Morayshire, Scotland.   Maritime Reconnaissance
HS/BAe Nimrod MR 2P   (18 airplanes pooled)
Motto: Endurance

No. 120 Squadron formed at Cramlington, on 1 January 1918, intended to join the Independent Force with D.H. 9A day bombers. But before the unit could move to France and become operational the Armistice was signed. The squadron subsequently received D. H. 10 which it used in the mail carrying and communications role until disbanding on 21 October, 1919. It reformed with Consolidated Liberators in June 1941, with Coastal Command and spent the next four years on operations over the Atlantic on anti-U-boat operations flying from bases in Northern Ireland and Iceland, sinking more U-boats than any other squadron. It remained in the maritime role post-war since October 1946, when No. 160 Squadron was re-numbered No. 120 Squadron operating Avro Lancaster GR.3, and successive marks of piston-engined Shackletons to the jet-powered HS Nimrod which it first received in October, 1970.

Declared operational on type in January 1971, in January 1977, the squadron assumed, new tasks such as anti-submarine warfare (ASW), surface surveillance, SAR, and patrol of the UKs 200 mile coastal fishery limits. The squadron sharing the tasking with the other No.18 Group Nimrod units. However, in October 1981, fishery protection duties were relinquished when they were assumed by the Ministry of Agriculture, Fisheries and Food, using PBN Islander and/or Dornier Do 228 aircraft (although Scottish Fisheries used two Reims/Cessna FR 182s fitted with a military Ferranti surveillance radar - later replaced with a cheaper to maintain civil Allied Signal equipment - only later to be changed back again). During 1981, the Nimrod crews converted to the up-dated MR.2s, which are currently being refurbished and upgraded to MR 2000 (MR 4) standard for use well into the 21 Century. Albeit, as is often the "norm" with UK commissioned military upgrades it is years behind schedule with the new aircraft (with new wings, avionics, search radar and engines) not scheduled to enter service until 2005 !

One of the saddest events in the No. 120 Squadrons history occurred on 2 September 1995, when Nimrod MR.2 (XV239) with all its experienced flight demonstration crew on board crashed into Lake Ontario, Canada, while taking part in the CNE Airshow at Toronto. The official findings of the air accident board resulting in pilot error..! Currently the squadron still operates as part of the Kinloss Wing, within No.3 Group, Strike Command with its H.Q. at Northwood, Middlesex.

Several Nimrods carry squadron markings but these are purely symbolic and do not indicate an association with a specific unit as all the airplanes at Kinloss are shared by the three front-line squadrons and the Nimrod conversion unit No. 42(R) Squadron. Currently (2002) the airplanes are in hemp finish and generally carry no markings except national low-viz roundels and stripes.

114.

No. 201 Squadron

RAF Kinloss, Morayshire, Scotland. Maritime Recce/ASW
HS/BAe Nimrod MR. 2P
Motto: *Hic et ubique* — 'Here and everywhere'

No. 201 Squadron's origins lay back in October, 1914, when it was commissioned as the first RNAS squadron to form, serving with distinction over France in WW I mainly in the fighter role. As No. 1 Squadron RNAS it was redesignated No. 201 Squadron RAF on 1 April, 1918, returning to the UK to deactivate in December, 1919. It reformed as a Supermarine Southampton flying-boat unit in January, 1929, later receiving the Saro London which was still in use at the outbreak of WW II. 1940, saw the arrival of Short Sunderland of which successive marks were used throughout the war, on maritime duties over the Atlantic, Norway and Biscay. No. 201 Squadron was in fact one of the last squadrons to operate the type until disbanding at Pembroke Dock on 28 February, 1957. It again reformed on 1 October 1958, when No. 220 Squadron was re-numbered No. 201 Squadron, this time equipped with Avro Shackleton maritime patrol planes, these operated until it became the first unit to equip with the jet-powered HS Nimrods in October, 1970.

The squadron has operated the Nimrod for thirty years, upgrading to the much improved MR.2 variant in 1981, having taken an active part in the Falklands campaign in the South Atlantic in 1982. A notable and unusual event on 11 August, 1988, occurred when a No. 201 Squadron Nimrod was scrambled from Kinloss to assist a small Cessna civil airplane which was some 400 miles off course through a navigational error and running out of fuel between Greenland and Iceland. The Nimrod guided the aircraft through dense cloud to ditch alongside Weather Station Lima. The year 2002 sees No.201 Squadron still based at Kinloss, flying the Nimrod with squadron operational aircraft drawn from pooled aircraft of the Central Servicing Wing as required with no unit markings carried.

'Mighty Hunter'
25 Years of Nimrod
(1969-1994)

No. 206 Squadron

RAF Kinloss, Morayshire, Scotland. Maritime reconnaissance
HS/BAe Nimrod MR. 2P
Motto: *Nihil nos effugit* - 'Nought escapes us'

No. 206 Squadron also began life as an RNAS squadron back in December, 1916, joining the RAF battle order on the 1 April, 1918, to spend several months in Germany as part of the occupying forces after the Armistice in November that year. A move to Egypt followed and in February 1920, it was renumbered No. 47 Squadron. Reformation occurred in June 1936, with Avro Anson I received followed by Lockheed Hudson in 1940, Boeing Fortresses in 1942 and Consolidated Liberators in 1944, all three types being deployed on Atlantic ASW patrols. Post-war the squadron spent a brief period as a transport unit before disbanding in April 1946, only to reappear again as a transport unit with Avro Yorks at Lyneham in November 1947, which it flew in the Berlin Airlift later re-equipping with Douglas Dakota until stood down in February, 1950.

Reformed at St Eval, Cornwall in September, 1952, the squadron equipped with the Avro Shackleton maritime patrol plane flying successive marks until re-equipping with the Nimrod MR. 1 in November, 1971. Upgrade to Nimrod M.R.2 occurred during 1981-82, with the type now being operated by the squadron for some thirty years in total, having deployed in the Falklands, the Gulf, and the Balkans. With the Nimrods currently being upgraded to M.R.4 standard the squadron can no doubt look forward to at least another thirty years on type. No squadron markings are carried, the unit using airplanes from the Kinloss Wing pool.

Nimrod MR2 on patrol over the North Sea flying from its Kinloss base in Scotland   (RAF)

HS Nimrod firing Sidewinder

117.

No. 22 Squadron

Search and Rescue (SAR)
Headquarters & 'A' Flight   RMB Chivenor, Devon (24 hour cover)
'B' Flight   AAC base Wattisham, Suffolk
'C' Flight   RAF Valley, Anglesey, Wales.
Westland Sea King HAR 3A (8 - two per flight)
Motto: *Preux et audacieux* - 'Valiant and Brave'
Nickname: 'Dinky Dos'

Formed at Gosport on 1 September 1915, No. 22 Squadron served throughout WW I as a two-seat fighter unit on the Western Front, initially with F. E. 2b and then the Bristol Fighter. Having become No. 22 Squadron RAF on 1 April 1918, it was the first of the new air forces units to carry out official missions. In the inter-war period the squadron was deployed on test and trials duties with the A&AEE at Martlesham Heath near Ipswich, until 1934, when it became a torpedo-bomber unit with Vickers Vildebeest. It continued in this role in WW II initially with the Bristol Beaufort in the UK and then in the Far East, where it eventually re-equipped with Bristol Beaufighters. Following a lengthy post-war disbandment the squadron reformed on 15 February 1955, in the search and rescue role with Westland Whirlwind HAR. 2 helicopters. In August 1962, the much improved Whirlwind H.A.R. 10 was received, greatly increasing the units capabilities and operability, which were much enhanced again, on receipt of the Westland Wessex H.A.R. 2s which supplemented the Whirlwinds in May 1976, replacing them completely by November 1981. Westland Wessex were used until July 1994, when they were supplanted by Westland Sea King H.A.R. 3/3As with which the squadron still operates today in the SAR role. Whilst the unit is primarily tasked for rescue of "downed" military crews it works closely with H.M. Coastguard and other civilian rescue services as and when needed.
The squadrons Sea Kings are finished in a bright overall yellow colour scheme, the Maltese cross, over which is superimposed the Greek character 'pi' (**n**) on a red disc encircled in white appears on the forward fuselage. RAF Rescue in black appears below the cockpit windows on both sides of the fuselage as does Royal Air Force above and Rescue below the rear fuselage observation blisters.

No 22 (SAR) Squadron Sea King HAR 3

No. 22 Squadron Sea King

119.

No. 202 Squadron

Search and Rescue (SAR)
Headquarters & 'A' Flight RAF Boulmer, Northumberland
'D' Flight RAF Lossiemouth, Moray, Scotland
'E' Flight RAF Leaconfield, Yorkshire
Westland Sea King HAR 3 (8 - two per flight)
Motto: *Semper Vigilant* - 'Always Vigilant'

Originally established as No. 2 Squadron RNAS, No. 202 Squadron came into being with the formation of the RAF in April 1918, and saw action on the Western Front during the closing stages of WW I with Airco D. H. 4/9 bombers, before disbanding in January 1920. Reformed in Malta early in 1929 following the renumbering of No. 481 Flight, the squadron flew Fairey IIIFs and Supermarine Scapa flying-boats for several years. At the start of WW II it was equipped with Saro London flying-boats at Gibraltar and flew these until re-equipped with with Consolidated Catalina in 1941, followed by Short Sunderland. A move to Northern Ireland in September 1944, saw re-equipment with Catalina IVs until deactivating in June 1945. The squadron reformed again in October 1946 as a meteorological research squadron, initially with H. P. Halifax Met. 6 and later with H. P. Hastings Met.1/Met.3. Disbanded in July 1964, it reformed again in September through the renumbering of No. 228 Squadron at RAF Leaconfield, Yorks, assuming the SAR role with Westland Whirlwind HAR 10 until supplanted by Sea King HAR. 3 the first of which were received in August 1978.

As a typical example of the intensity of operations for the SAR units in December 1993, it was revealed that RAF, RN and HM Coastguard helicopters and mountain rescue teams between them had assisted a total of 1,473 people in distress in the British Isles during 1993 alone. With the busiest unit being "D" Flight of No.202 Squadron based at RAF Leuchars, Scotland. The fourteen SAR units around the UK had been called out by the RAF Rescue Co-ordination Centres at Edinburgh and Plymouth, on no less than 2,150 occasions. Increased use of NVGs meant that more rescues at night were carried out by RAF crews. In 1995 similar figures were recorded with a total of 1,300 people rescued by the rescue units and requests for assistance logged at 2,250 calls represented the highest ever. Indeed in December 1995, "D" Flight of No.202 Squadron broke its own call-out record for one year with a total of 247. The previous highest call-outs being 241 in 1992. Ironically it was to be "D" Flight again to set a new call-out record on 22 December 1999, when it logged a total of 273 call outs for the year.

With the squadron now fully equipped with seven upgraded HAR 3A Sea Kings there is no doubt that there is every chance the call out record will again be broken by one of the squadrons Flights now variously located at RAF Boulmer, Northumberland (H.Q. & "A" Flt), RAF Lossiemonth, Moray ("D" Flt), and RAF Leaconfield, Yorks ("E" Flt) with No.202 Squadron remaining a major provider of search and rescue services by day and by night. No. 202 Squadrons SAR Helicopters are in overall yellow livery with the same RAF markings in black as No. 22 SAR Squadron, with the squadron's badge a mallard alighting, on a white disc, prominently displayed on the sides of the forward fuselage.

No. 203(R) Squadron

RAF St Mawgan, Westland Sea King OCU
Westland Sea King HAR 3A (3)
Motto: *Occidens Oriensque* — 'West and East'

No. 3 (Naval), later No. 203 Squadron (RAF) formed originally as 'C' Squadron in November 1911, at Eastchurch, as the first Naval Air Unit. Having served in support of the ill-fated Gallipoli expedition in 1915, the squadron was absorbed into the newly formed RAF on 1 April 1918, equipped with Sopwith Camels. Based on the Western Front, in France, it flew fighter and ground attack missions until the end of the war. Reduced to a cadre in March 1919, it returned to the UK and disbanded on 21 January 1920, although within three months it had reformed as a fleet fighter squadron again with Sopwith Camels and later Nieuport Nightjars. Which although designed as a single-seat deck-landing fighter was used as a land fighter by No. 203 Squadron during the Chanak Crisis in the latter months of 1922 in Turkey. On the 1 April 1923, the squadron was split to become Nos. 401 and 402 (Fleet Fighter) Flights. But on 1 January 1929, No 482 (Coastal Reconnaissance) Flight at Mount Batten, Plymouth, was redesignated No. 203 Squadron and on 28 February 1929, it left for Iraq with three Supermarine Southampton flying boats. Arriving in mid-March 1929, patrols over the Persian Gulf commenced, with re-equipment with Short Rangoons in April 1931, making No. 203 Squadron the only RAF flying-boat unit in Iraq.

In 1934, three of the squadrons airplanes made an historic "cruise" from Basrah in Iraq to Melbourne, Australia and back. Only six Short Rangoons were built for the RAF, and these were taken to Aden in 1935, during the Abyssinian Crisis before being passed on to No. 210 Squadron in the UK in September 1935, when No. 203 Squadron converted to Short Singapore III with official code PP-. The squadron returned to Iraq in August 1936, returning to Aden again at the start of WW II in September 1939. Conversion to Bristol Blenheim Is commenced in December 1939, with the squadron receiving its own airplanes in March 1940. With Italy's entry into the war in June 1940, the squadrons Blenheims flew reconnaissance and fighter patrols over the Red Sea until 1941. When it moved to Egypt and Palestine. Following the Syrian campaign the squadron began flying reconnaissance missions over the Eastern Mediterranean receiving some Martin Maryland B.Is from No. 39 Squadron in February 1942. Martin Baltimores with their more powerful 1,660-hp Wright Double-Row Cyclone engines were added in August 1942 and by November that year the squadron was fully equipped with the type. In November 1943, No. 203 Squadron moved to India converting to Vickers Wellington G.R. 8 for coastal patrol duties which were replaced by American Consolidated Liberator G.R. 6, G.R. 8 with official code CJ-, for anti-shipping patrols flown from Ceylon in February 1945 until the wars end.

Following a period of transport duties in South-East Asia, No. 203 Squadron returned to the UK in May 1946, converting to Avro Lancaster B.3 also coded CJ- followed successively by the Lancaster G.R.3, M.R.3, and A.S.R.3 variants for maritime patrol and ASR (Air Sea Rescue) duties. These converted WW II bombers were flown from RAF Leuchars, Scotland, until the unit moved to RAF Topcliffe, Yorks, in January 1953, when it converted to the maritime Lockheed Neptune M.R. I (coded B-) which remained in service with the squadron until it disbanded on 1 September 1956.

Just over two years later on 1 November 1958, No. 240 Squadron at RAF Ballykelly, Northern Ireland, was renumbered No. 203 Squadron equipped with maritime patrol Avro Shackleton successively operating all variants until January 1972. When relocated to Malta conversion to the jet HS Nimrod MR.1 began in July 1971, but as problems arose over the use of the Maltese bases No. 203 Squadron moved to the NATO base at Signonella, Sicily, only to return Malta again in April 1972, where it remained until disbandment in December 1977. The No. 203 number-plate then lay dormant for almost twenty years until resurrected when the new Westland Sea King HAR 3A OCU was established at RAF St Mawgan, Cornwall, in 1996. Currently the squadrons Sea King HAR 3As carry a green sea horse on a white circle as the unit emblem.

Sea King of No 203(R) Squadron Sea King OCU

No. 1 (F) Squadron

RAF Cottesmore, Rutland. Joint RN/RAF Unit.
MDC/BAe Harrier GR 7 (12) plus 1 T.10
Motto : *In omnibus princeps* - 'First in all things'
Nickname : 'Shiny Firsts'

No. 1

No. 1 Squadron traces its history back to 1878, when it formed in the British Army as a balloon unit assuming the title No. 1 Airship Company, at Farnborough in May, 1912. Until late 1913 it operated lighter-than-air machines, but on transferring its airships to the Navy on 1 January 1914, it was renamed No. 1 Squadron RFC in May 1914, at Brooklands, Surrey, with an assortment of airplanes under its first C.O., Major C. A. M. Longcroft. In 1916, No. 1 Squadron was subsequently assigned to fighter duties, a role in which it has continued ever since either in the fighter or ground-attack capacity. During WW II it saw action in France with the Hawker Hurricane and took part in the Battle of Britain before being re-assigned to night fighter operations in 1941-42. Re-equipping with Hawker Typhoon, it turned its attention to the strike role for the closing stages of WW II and did not revert to fighter duties until after the war when it returned to RAF Tangmere in the south of England. Transferred to RAF Stradishall near Newmarket, Suffolk, after the closure of Tangmere, the squadron underwent a role change assuming fighter ground-attack duties with its Hawker Hunter FGA 9s, which it operated until shortly before moving to RAF Wittering in 1969, to become the world's first operational VTOL strike fighter unit with Hawker Siddeley Harrier GR. 1/1A.

Having flown the type on a number of Strike Command exercises and numerous operational detachments to Belize, Central America, six Harrier GR 1s were detached to reinforce the British garrison as the border situation with Guatemala worsened. Although the aircraft were soon withdrawn they returned again in July 1977, following another rise in tension in the area. In 1982 the squadrons GR. 3s joined elements of the Royal Navy's FRS.1 Sea Harrier Force aboard HMS *Hermes* in the war in the South Atlantic against the Argentinians over the sovereignty of the Malvinas/Falkland Islands. Later No.1s Harriers operated from an advance base using a temporary metal airstrip at San Carlos. For ground attack, the GR.3s used cluster weapons and carried a 3,000 lb bomb-load. 150 missions were flown by the squadron, with two aircraft lost to heavy A.A. fire at Goose Green.

Pilots of No. 1(F) Squadron were converted to the Harrier GR. Mk. 5 by the Harrier Conversion Team, and the unit received its first GR. 5s on 23 November 1988, withdrawing the last of its first-generation Harrier GR 3s on 31 March, 1989. During a detachment to RAF Valley in July 1989, the new Harrier GR.5s of No.1 Squadron were the first RAF operational aircraft to carry out live firings of the AIM-9L Sidewinder AAM. In the autumn of 1989 No.1 Squadron became the first Harrier unit to undertake the night attack role, subsequently becoming cleared for NVG operations. The squadron was re-declared as operational to NATO on 2 November, 1989. Following conversion to GR. 7, from and was the first front-line RAF Harrier unit to work up in the night attack role, from the autumn of 1989. Initially assigned to SACUER's Strategic Reserve, No. 1(F) Squadron was subsequently assigned to NATO's RF(Air), declared operational on 1 January 1996.

Unmarked low-viz Harrier releases AIM 9 Sidewinder missile

125.

From the 67th, GR.5 production aircraft, the enhanced aircraft received the designation GR.7. Subsequently all the initial builds were retrofitted to GR.7 standard which entered operational service with No.1 Squadron in November 1992.

Since the Gulf War, No.1 Squadron has undertaken regular detachments in support of Operations *Warden* and *Grapple* and has deployed aircraft aboard the RN carrier HMS *Illustrious* for joint operations with the Royal Navy's Sea Harriers. This exercise proved expedient when in November 1997, seven No.1 Squadron Harrier GR.7s were flown to join HMS *Invincible* in the Mediterranean as part of the operational air group on standby to move to the Gulf in the event of a UN decision to mount new air strikes against Iraq.

In January 1998, No.1 Squadron kept to its tradition of "sailing" into combat when it embarked HMS *Invincible* en-route for operations related to renewed troubles in the Gulf. Later live-armed operational missions over Bosnia were also undertaken, flying from the Italian air force base at Gioia del Colle. A year later in April 1999 on the 50th Anniversary of NATO, No.1 Squadron under C.O Gp Capt Andre Dezonie, was in the front line again in support of Operation "Allied Force", supplying crews and aircraft operating from Aviano AB, Italy over Kosovo against FYR forces, and flew missions over the Yugoslav capital, Belgrade. The squadron was heavily involved in the initial raids which commenced on 24 March 1999, when Paveway II 1,000 lb laser-guided bombs were used.

Currently No.1 Squadron is based at RAF Cottesmore, Rutland, with its Harrier GR.7s and a dual-seat T.10 trainer on strength co-located with Nos 3 and 4 Harrier squadrons, to be joined in 2003, by Nos 800 and 801 Sea Harrier F/A-2 Squadrons of the Fleet Air Arm from RNAS Yeovilton, to bring the units of the Joint Harrier Strike Force (inaugurated 2000) together at one base. Command of the unit will alternate between the navy and the air force at set intervals. Further in 2002, it has been announced that the Royal Navy Sea Harrier fleet is to be withdrawn from use in 2007, and could be sold to India along with the carrier HMS *Invincible* to help offset the cost of the supersonic F-35 VTOL strike plane on order from Lockheed Martin.

Aircraft Markings and Codes

Official markings were not carried by No. 1 Squadron airplanes until 1917, when Nieuport Scouts started carrying large individual letters and a vertical stripe aft of the fuselage roundel. This was changed to sloping white lines on each side of the roundel on S. E. 5As, although within a month the lines were replaced by a hollow white circle aft of the roundel.

No markings were carried on Sopwith Snipes but they were re-introduced with A.W. Siskin airplanes in 1927, when two horizontal red stripes appeared in parallel in front of the fuselage roundel tapering to a point aft of it. These markings were retained on Hawker Furies. Similar red stripes were painted across the full span of the upper mainplane. Propeller spinners and wheel centres were painted red. Later the flight commanders airplanes was also painted in Flight colours and a winged figure "1" was painted on a white spearhead on a red tail-fin.

In late 1938, all the squadrons airplanes were camouflaged and all markings were removed. Soon after Hawker Hurricanes were received with the official unit code letters NA- were applied. In September 1939, standard day fighter colours; yellow wing leading edges and sky-blue spinner and sky-blue identification band aft of the roundel were applied, with the official unit code changed to JX- that was used throughout the war and carried over to the Gloster Meteor jets.

In 1950, the precursor of the modern day markings were used when the codes were replaced with a red-edged white rectangle on each side of the fuselage roundel. On the Hawker Hunters the markings were moved to the sides of the nose and consisted of a white disc on which was a winged red "1" flanked by red outlined white triangles. Aircraft code letters were on the fin in white. The same markings have been used on Harrier jump jets but individual aircraft identification has varied between numerals and letters. Currently a red and white winged number '1' on a white diamond is carried on the forward variable nozzle casing on light-blue/grey coloured airplanes.

No. 3 Squadron

RAF Cottesmore, Rutland. Offensive Support
MDC/BAe Harrier GR 7 (12) plus 1 T.10
Motto :   *Tertius primus erit* - 'The third shall be first'

Established at Larkhill, Salisbury Plain, on 13 May, 1912, No. 3 Squadron was a reconnaissance unit until becoming a fighter unit with Sopwith Camel in WW I. It retained the role between the wars stationed at RAF Kenley and saw extensive service as a fighter unit in WW II destroying a total of 288 V 1 flying bombs operating from bases in both the UK and France. It ended the war in Germany where it remained until returning to the UK in May, 1999. Having successively operated such types as the D. H. Vampire, Canadair Sabre (F-86) F. 4, Hawker Hunter, Gloster Javelin and EE Canberra, in the interdiction role.

It flew the Canberra B(I)8 for eleven years until 1 January 1972 from Geilenkirchen and Laarbruch before moving to Wildenrath on that date, converting to the successive marks of Harrier in the tactical reconnaissance and strike role. In March 1977, the unit moved to Gutersloh with the Harrier GR.3 receiving the much improved GR.5 from September 1989. Converting to the MDC/BAe GR.7 since 1991. Following the closure of Guterslohn during 1992, No.3 Squadron was again based at Laarbruch which itself closed mid-1999 with No.3 Squadron returning to RAF Cottesmore, Rutland on 11 May 1999. Laarbruch which throughout its life since it was built in 1954, has always been an RAF base, is likely to become a civil cargo airport.

Since re-equipping with the Harrier GR-7 the squadron has provided aircraft on rotation to help police the northern no-fly zone in Iraq, flying from the famous Turkish AB, at Incirlik. February 1998, saw No.3 Squadron as with No.1 Squadron before them forge closer relationships with the FAAs Sea Harrier F/A 2 units when six Harrier GR 7s, twelve pilots and 100 ground personnel embarked the aircraft carrier HMS *Illustrious* in the Mediterranean. Later, moving to form part of the Joint Harrier Strike Force 2000 to be based at RAF Cottesmore from 2003. In March/April 1999, as with the rest of the Harrier force No.3 Squadron was engaged in the NATO operations in Kosovo.

Two Harrier GR 7s and a BAe Hawk on the flight line. Nos 1 & 20 Squadron

Aircraft Markings and Codes

Unit markings were not carried on No. 3 Squadron airplanes until they re-equipped with Sopwith Camel scouts in October 1917, two vertical white bars just aft the roundels. These were later changed in December 1917, to one each side of the roundel and in March 1918, to two bars just forward of the tailplane. After the first World War the squadron's airplanes did not carry any special markings until 1924, when the silver painted Sopwith Snipes appeared with a broad green stripe down each side of the fuselage from the propeller to the rudder post and across the upper wing. These markings were retained until the arrival of the camouflaged Hawker Hurricane fighter. On reverting to the camouflaged Gloster Gladiator biplanes in July 1938, the official unit code OP- was used and individual airplane letter codes were also carried. Replacement Hawker Hurricanes also carried the OP- code changing to QO- in August 1939, this code being used until June 1944, when the Hawker Tempest Vs were re-coded JF-.

In 1946, the official unit code changed again to J5- with some airplanes carrying a badge on the fin. Silver-painted De Havilland Vampire Is carried the code "5" on the nose and Vampire FB. 5s the same number on the booms. In 1950, the codes were deleted and the individual airplane letter was repeated on the nose. Later the fin 'acorn' fairings were painted the traditional leaf-green colour and the 2nd TAF (Germany) code "A" was added on the booms. These markings were retained on camouflaged airplanes.

On receiving Canadair F-86 Sabres, markings were confined to leaf green engine intakes then later camouflaged airplanes changed to green rectangles edged in gold on each side of the fuselage roundels with individual airplane letters on the fin also with gold outlining. Hawker Hunters were similarly marked. The Gloster Javelin all-weather night fighters saw the introduction of a red and grey cocktrice on a white disc superimposed on a green band across the fin, the individual code being in white. The EE Canberra light bomber and the VSTOL Harrier retained these markings, although the green bands were not carried by the Canberras until they had been in service for a number of years. On Harriers the markings were moved to the sides of the nose. On the GR 5 variant and currently on the squadron's GR 7 airplanes they appear forward of the front vectored thrust nozzle casing and aft of the intake.

Harrier GR. 5 and GR. 7 colour schemes :

The first two development batch Harrier GR 5s wore a grey colour scheme, but series airplanes used the dark green colours trialled by No. 3 Squadron From late-1992, serial numbers were raised slightly on the rear fuselage to keep them free of soot and other deposits from the rear nozzles. When operations in the predominantly medium-level role over Northern Iraq commenced, Harriers deployed on Operation *Warden* received a a temporary coat of grey ARTF (Acrylic Removable Temporary Finish), which gave way to a permanent two-tone grey finish using LIR (Low Infra-Red) signature paint, with Dark Camouflage Grey topsides and Medium Sea Grey undersurfaces. National insignia reverted to dark blue and dark red and serials reverted to their normal size. At almost the same time, individual airplane identification codes within the squadrons were replaced by a uniform, fleet-wide system consisting of two-digit numeral codes - these being derived from the airplanes original BAe constructors numbers. On both grey colour schemes, roundels were carried above the port wing (and on the intakes) only, and not above the starboard wing. The dual-seat T. 10 training planes have so far remained in their original green finish.

MDC/BAe Harrier GR 7 line-up

Combat-capable dual-seat Harrier T.10

No. IV (AC) Squadron

RAF Cottesmore, Rutland. Offensive Support
MDC/BAe Harrier GR 7 (12) plus 1 T.10
Motto : *In futurum videre* - 'To see into the future'

Initially formed in 1912, at Farnborough, No. 4 Squadron served as a reconnaissance squadron on the Western Front throughout the war, later during the closing stages with R. E. 8. It was retained in the post-war battle order and operated a variety of types including the Bristol Fighter, A. W. Atlas, and Hawker Audax biplanes, but these had been replaced by the high-winged Westland Lysander monoplane by the beginning of WW II, the squadron being deployed to France on army co-operation duties and later air-sea-rescue duties along the East Coast when withdrawn to the UK. Re-equipment with Curtiss Tomahawk and North American Mustangs saw a change to tactical reconnaissance duties. By 1944, when the squadron returned to France, it had re-equipped with Supermarine Spitfire and D. H. Mosquitoes for offensive operations. Retained in Germany, after the war the squadron operated numerous fighter, fighter-bomber types including the D. H. Mosquito, D. H. Vampire FB. 5 and FB. 9, Sabre F. 4 and Hawker Hunter F. 4/F. 6, until becoming a tactical photographic reconnaissance unit with the Supermarine Swift FR. 5, Hunter PR. 10 and FGA.9, until receiving HS Harrier GR. 1/3s in April 1970.

No. IV (AC) Squadron converted straight from the GR. 3 variant to the vastly improved GR.7 from September 1990,though it was to be eighteen months before a squadron airplane would fly a representative operational night sortie and it was the last Harrier unit to actually train for the night attack role. It is still operational on type more than ten years later currently based at RAF Cottesmore, Rutland, to where it moved in 1999. With the formerly permanently resident No.1417 Flight (Harrier GR.3) having left Belize on 8 July 1993, on 6 September 1993, No. IV Squadron deployed four Harrier GR.7 airplanes to the colony for a month, demonstrating effective reinforcements could be quickly draw from the UK if necessary. In January 1995, on their fourth deployment to Incirlik,Turkey, as part of Operation *Warden* to protect the Kurds in Northern Iraq a sortie of four Harrier GR.7s of No.4 Squadron passed the landmark of 5,000 operational hours flown in the region since they had taken over from the Sepecat Jaguar units in April 1993. Until in April 1995, the deployments tasking was taken over for the first time by six Panavia Tornado IDS variants. On the 24 July 1995, No. 4 Squadron despatched its first five aircraft to Gioia del Colle, Italy, with a further seven sent on 1 August, with this initial detachment reduced to nine aircraft after the squadron had been brought up to operational readiness. No IV was the first RAF Harrier unit to provide aircraft for Operation *Deny Flight* over the former Yugoslavia. Later, during Operation *Deliberate Force,* the squadron flew operational sorties dropping 454-kg (1,000 lb) LGBs with Sepecat Jaguar airplanes providing target designation.

No IV (AC) Squadron was based at RAF Laarbruch, Germany, until its return to the UK on the 13 April 1999, to form the basis of the new joint RN/RAF Harrier Strike 2000 Facility at RAF Cottesmore, Rutland in 2003. In preparation for this, in September 1999, No IV Squadron carried out its first carrier landings during a two-week deployment aboard HMS *Illustrious*. In 1999/2000 No. 4 Squadron still based four Harriers at Gioia del Colle in, Italy, in support of Operation *Engadine* the NATO-led peace plan, in Kosovo.

Aircraft Markings and Codes

In 1916, No. IV Squadron's B.E. 2cs had a white band around the fuselage forward of the roundels. R. E. 8s were similarly marked except for "A" Flight airplanes that during early 1918, when operating independently were marked with three white bands on the underside of the rear fuselage. After the war Bristol F 2bs initially appeared with the white band painted aft of the roundels but when all-over silver aircraft were used all unit markings were deleted. With the arrival of Hawker Audax biplanes a large figure "4" was carried on the fuselage sides between the gunners cockpit and the roundel with the army co-operation "six-point star" badge on the fin. Hawker Hectors employed the unit badge superimposed on a six-point star as fin markings. Westland Lysanders were similarly marked, but also carried the official unit code TV- changed to FY- in May, 1939. In September 1939, the code reverted to TV-, although from 1943, no unit codes were carried.

D. H. Mosquito PR XVIs and Supermarine Spitfire PR XIs were painted all-over in "PR-blue" with small white serials and individual aircraft code letters. With the re-numbering of No. 605 Squadron to No. 4 Squadron at Celle, in September,1945, with D. H. Mosquito FB VIs the unit code UP- was retained, initially painted in dull red, bur later in royal-blue with gold outline. Initially D. H. Vampire FB Vs carried the UP- code but this was soon replaced by 2nd TAF unit coded "B" and individual airplane identification letters. F-86 Sabres received similar markings the letters in white, flanking the fuselage roundel, painted black and red, the colours divided by a yellow lightning flash. The aircraft code was moved forward of the unit markings, and the fin badge was retained.

Hawker Hunters used the same format, although the stylized badge was moved to the sides of the nose and white individual airplane codes were applied to the fin. Shortly before the squadron disbanded relinquishing its Hunter FR 10s for HS Harrier GR 1s the large markings flanking the roundels were removed and similar smaller markings were applied either side of the stylized nose emblem. These markings were applied to the Harriers with individual aircraft letterings in yellow on the fin. Currently 2002 squadron airplanes carry a yellow lightning flash inside a red and black circle flanked by bars the forward thrust vectoring nozzle casing on either side of the fuselage. A yellow lightning flash on a red and black stripe appears at the top of the fin.

A typical early operational RAF (Germany) Harrier colour scheme is shown on this No 4 Squadron GR. 1 variant, currently on display at the *Luftwaffenmuseum* at the former RAF base at Gatow, Berlin, scene of the renowned Berlin Airlift.

No. 20(R) Squadron

RAF Wittering, Northants. No. 233 Harrier OCU
MDC/BAe Harrier GR 7 (9) Plus T. 10 (5)
Motto: *Facta non verba* - 'Deeds not words'
Nickname: 'Double Crossers'

No. 20

No. 20 Squadron formed on 1 September, 1915, at Netheravon as a two-seat fighter unit for service on the Western Front and was the RFC's top-scoring unit of WW I. Post-war it moved to India where it flew on policing duties and border patrols with the Bristol Fighter. At the start of WW II the squadron was still stationed in India and took part in the Burma campaign with the Hawker Hurricane II and Supermarine Spitfires. Disbanded on 31 July 1947, in India the squadron reformed at Llanbedr, in Wales, flying a variety of types on army co-operation and target-towing duties before re-forming for fighter duties with the 2nd TAF in Germany in 1952, successively operating D. H. Vampire and Venom fighter-bombers, the Canadair F. 4 Sabre which were later replaced by successive marks of the Hunter culminating with the FGA 9 variant which were flown for nearly ten years from September 1961, to February 1970. At Tengah in defence of Singapore, with a Flight of Scottish Pioneer CC.1 taken on charge briefly in 1969, for forward air control duties in relation to the squadrons associated tasks with Operation *Firedog* in Malaya.

Returning to Wildenrath, RAF Germany in December, 1970, the squadron re-equipped with the VTOL HS Harrier GR 1/3 until converting to the Sepecat Jaguar in late 1976. In May 1984, No. 20 Squadron became the RAF's third Panavia Tornado GR 1 squadron based at RAF Laarbruch joining Nos. XV and 16 Squadrons to form the Laarbruch Wing. However, following the Gulf War No. 20 Squadron's number-plate was taken over as a shadow identity by No. 233 OCU the Harrier Conversion Unit at RAF Wittering, where it remains today with its compliment of single-seat GR 7 and T.10 dual-seat training planes. Albeit with reserve squadron status in the 21st Century battle order.

No 20 Squadron OCU Harrier GR 7 with in-flight refuelling probe extended

Aircraft markings and codes.

It is believed No. 20 Squadron's F.E. 2bs carried no unit markings but the Bristol Fighters used a single vertical white bar forward of the fuselage roundel. In India, the Bristol Fighters carried individual letters and, at one stage, the numerals '20' appeared on the fin. Later the squadrons airplanes had a coloured band denoting the Flight painted around the fuselage, this marking retained on Westland Wapitis which also had chequered stripes across the upper mainplane centre sections and individual identification letters on a square panel aft of the fuselage roundel.

Hawker Audax airplanes continued with coloured bands and some airplanes carried the eagle badge on the fin. Following the Munich Crisis of 1938, the official two-letter code PM- was allocated but probably not carried, although the new HN- code did appear on the squadron's Hawker Audax and Westland Lysanders from September 1939. Hawker Hurricanes and Supermarine Spitfires were unmarked apart from the individual airplane letters, but the HN- code was affixed to Hawker Tempests. Airplanes flown at Llanbedr on target-towing duties carried the TH- code, but when the unit reformed in Germany with the 2nd TAF, red and blue diamonds on a green background, was applied on each side of the boom roundel, this later changed to red, white and green horizontal bars before the Vampires were withdrawn from use. The squadron's Canadair Sabres and Hawker Hunters carried similar markings, with the Sabres also having the squadron eagle on a white shield painted on the sides of the nose, and like the Hunters the airplane letters were carried on the fin.

In the Far East, on Hawker Hunters the centre-piece of the badge was carried on a light-blue disc on the nose, flanked by the 'fighter style' red, white and green bars on a light-blue background. This same style of marking was carried over to the Harrier jump jets, and the Sepecat Jaguar, where it appeared on the engine air intakes and later on the Panavia Tornado on either side of the forward fuselage roundel beneath the pilots cockpit. Except on the Tornado the green bar segment was dropped and the squadron eagle on a white disc in a blue circle appeared on the sides of the intake ducts. Individual airplane letters were carried on the fins of these airplanes, supplemented by the unit code 'C' on later service entry Jaguars and 'G' on Tornados in the series GA to GZ.

On assuming Harrier OCU responsibilities in September 1992, currently (2002) the units Harriers carry the squadrons eagle on a white disc flanked by a white stripe on a blue background on the forward thrust vectoring nozzle casing. High on the tail-fin is a stripe made up of black, yellow, green and red triangles with a black Lynxs head on a white disc on the fin in front of an elongated sloping white rectangle between it, and the national red and blue stripes, these representative of No. 233 OCU

No. 20 Squadron Harrier GR 7 taking off on grass strip, with nose-wheel light ablaze

(RAF)

No. 800 Squadron (FAA)   RAF Cottesmore, Rutland,
No. 801 Squadron (FAA)   Joint RN/RAF Harrier Strike Force 2000 (Joint Force Harrier)
                              BAe Sea Harrier F/A 2 (7-9 airplanes per squadron)
No. 899 Squadron (FAA OCU/OEU)   RAF Wittering (Sea Harrier F/A 2 & T 8N)

The decision to develop a maritime version of the RAF's Harrier GR 3 was taken by the UK Government on 15 May, 1975. Designated Sea Harrier FRS. 1 the prototype flew on 20 August, 1978 and the first airplane was handed over to the Fleet Air Arm on 18 June, 1979. An Intensive Flying Trials Unit (IFTU), No 700A Squadron was formed at RNAS Yeovilton on 26 June 1979, to introduce the type into service. Later re-designated No. 899 Squadron in times of intense operational activities has supplied planes and crews for front-line operations. As in the Falklands when No. 809 Squadron was temporarily reformed on 8 April 1982. On 17 December the unit disbanded again and its airplanes were distributed between the three remaining squadrons.

The first operational Sea Harrier unit to form was No. 800 Squadron on 31 March, 1980 at Yeovilton, followed by No. 801 Squadron on 28 January 1981. Both units who were normally carrier-based No. 800 Squadron aboard HMS *Invincible* and No. 801 Squadron aboard HMS *Ark Royal* soon found themselves in action in the South Atlantic during the Falklands Conflict and subsequently in the Gulf War and the Balkan Conflicts, mainly carrying out CAP (Combat Air Patrol) in the regions.

In 1985, a mid-life update was initiated to refine the airplane to make it more combat capable. This gave rise to the Sea Harrier F/A 2 the first of two prototypes flying in September, 1988. It is of interest despite the addition of an additional equipment bay and a re-contoured nose to house the Ferranti Blue Vixen pulse doppler radar, the F/A 2 is actually 0.61 m (2 feet) shorter in overall length due to the elimination of the FRS 1s pitot probe. On the 7 December 1988, a contract was awarded to British Aerospace for the conversion of 31 FRS 1s to FRS 2 standard, this designation later changed to F/A 2. Carrier qualification trials were completed during November, 1990. Later in January 1994, a further contract was issued for ten new build F/A 2s. Three two-seat T. Mk 4N trainers were also brought to FRS 2 standard less the radar, and were redesignated T. Mk 8Ns.

Having joined forces with the RAF's Harrier fleet, it was determined the Sea Harrier would need further upgrades including an uprated engine to bring it to a similar standard as the RAF GR 9, at a cost of several millions of pounds. Subsequently with sixty Lockheed Martin F-35 supersonic Joint Strike Fighters on order for the Royal Navy it has been decided that in the short term the Sea Harriers should be withdrawn from use between 2004 and 2006, with the upgraded RAF GR 9s to operate from the Royal Navy's carriers as and when required. A decision which not unexpectedly has been greeted with some scepticism by some RAF Harrier pilots most of whom did not join the RAF to go to sea ! The British MoD has stated these measures are necessary to help offset to some degree the cost of the F-35 and the two new aircraft carriers intended for service entry in 2012.

BAe Sea Harrier F/A 2 with distinctive
nose radome housing powerful
Ferranti Blue Vixsen radar

134.

Unmarked FAA SEa Harrier F/A 2 '716' on combat air patrol in the Adriatic

Stablemate '717' F/A 2 in its 'hide' at Farnborough Air Salon. Shades of Joint Harrier Strike Force 2000

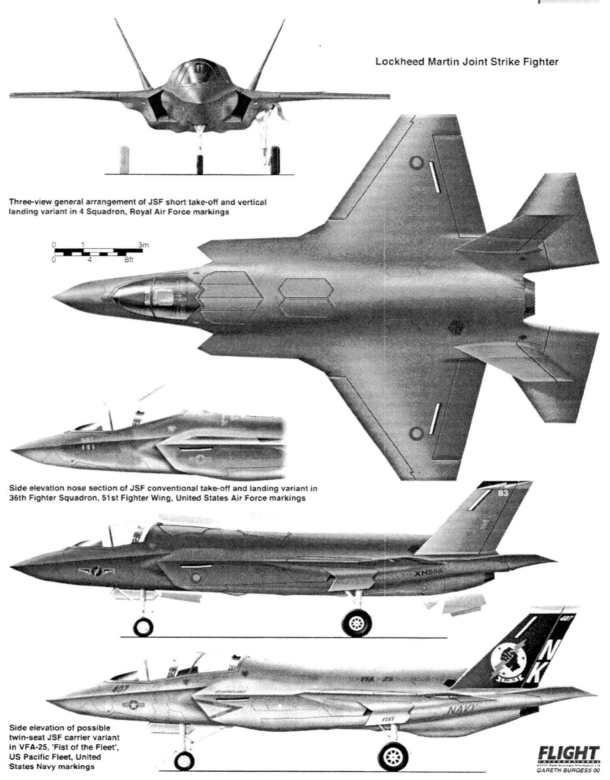

Lockheed Martin Joint Strike Fighter

Three-view general arrangement of JSF short take-off and vertical
landing variant in 4 Squadron, Royal Air Force markings

Side elevation nose section of JSF conventional take-off and landing variant in
36th Fighter Squadron, 51st Fighter Wing, United States Air Force markings

Side elevation of possible
twin-seat JSF carrier variant
in VFA-25, 'Fist of the Fleet',
US Pacific Fleet, United
States Navy markings

FLIGHT
GARETH BURGESS 00

136.

Personnel and Training Command   H. Q. RAF Innsworth, Gloucestershire.

Personnel and Training Command came into being on 1 April 1994, for recruiting and training of all regular and reserve personnel, officers and men. Its main areas of responsibilities include:

1. Maintain manpower levels
2. Provide non-operational flying training and ground crew training.
3. Medical and associated services
4. Chaplain and religious services
5. Accounts, security, welfare, and ceremonial duties
6. Finance and all expenditure associated with FTC.

As well as the staff colleges at RAF Cranwell and RAF Bracknell, with the Commandant at Cranwell responsible for the Air Cadets, and the University Air Squadrons, now equipped with Grob Tutor and Viking T.1 motorised gliders.

Pilot training for the RAF will often begin with university students who take up flying the Grob Tutor at one of the fifteen University Air Squadrons and Air Cadet Experience Flights on the Grob Vigilant T.1. On average about one third of the pilot intake comes from this source and by the time the students leave University to join the RAF some can have logged some 90 or more flying hours. Others may have done a minimum of 30 flyings hours will go to the Joint Elementary Flying Training School (JEFTS) at RAF Barkston Heath, Lincs. Where Hunting Contract Services operates the tri-service *abinito* trainers using a fleet (40) of civil-registered Slingsby T67M Firefly IIs and T67M-260s, with detachments at RAF Cranwell, Church Fenton, and the Army School of Flying at Middle Wallop.

G-Hong Slingsby T-67M was purchased by Hunting Engineering for use at the Barkstone Heath, Lincs Joint RN/RAF Evaluation Unit

137.

Air Cadets 'Air Experience' Grob T.I. Viking powered glider

This initial course of flying determines whether the candidates are suitable for more advanced flying training. Those deemed suitable for further training move on the Shorts Tucano at No. 1 FTS RAF Linton on Ouse, near York, while ex-UAS students move on to type at No. 3 FTS at RAF Cranwell, Lincs.

Shorts Tucano in standard FTS colours

Shorts Tucano in controversial 'gloss-black' finish

After basic training students are streamed for fast jet, multi-engine or helicopter, depending on their aptitude. Back-to-back fast jet training is undertaken at No. 4 FTS at RAF Valley, Anglesey. No. 4 FTS provides advanced, fixed wing flying training and weapons instruction on the superb BAe Hawk T1/T1A. It operates two squadrons, Nos. 19(R) and 208(R) with the airplanes pooled. No 19 Squadron also supports the Hawks operated by the Central Flying School (CFS) at Cranwell. Back-to-back training means all the student pilots advance and operational flying training is completed on the same course, before moving on to an OCU within Strike Command.

Looking to the future it is likely up to thirty BAe Hawk 100 series airplanes will be procured as LIFT (Lead In Fighter Trainers), for the Eurofighter pilots. The airplane equipped with the latest all-electronic cockpit as will be the premise of the Eurofighter pilot.

Gloss black finish Sidewinder-equipped BAe Hawk T 1A of No. 4 Flying Training School

No. 19

It is of interest that the black gloss finish as currently applied to Tucano and Hawk training planes is under question as there have been a number of near-miss incidents. It is thought the black colour scheme is best suited against a clear blue sky, but in the oft overcast UK countryside or over the lakes of Cumbria it is only marginally easier to see than a conventionally camouflaged airplane.

Sidewinder-equipped BAe Hawk T. 1A

141.

BAE Systems Hawk 100 LIFT (Lead in Fighter Trainer) with wing-tip Sidewinders fitted

(BAe)

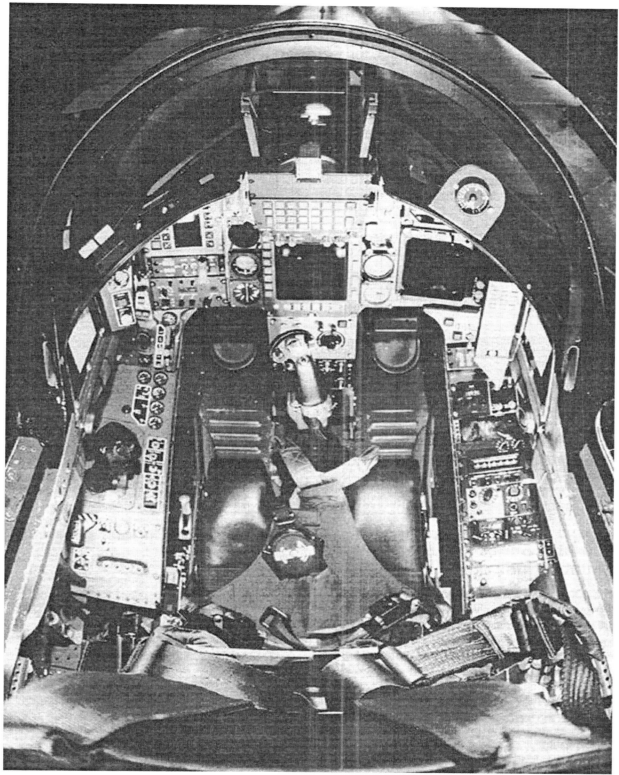

BAe Hawk 100 Series Cockpit   (BAe)

143.

The 'Welsh Dragon' from No. 4 FTS RAF Valley, Anglesey, North Wales

A low-viz Hawk T.1A (222) of No. 1 Tactical Weapons Unit carrying the 'shadow' markings of No. 79 Squadron (disbanded)

Symmetry in the sky.. the Red Arrows BAe Hawk T.1s

No. 74 "Tiger" Squadron the first to introduce the controversial gloss black colour scheme (the unit subsequently disbanded

Camouflaged Hawk T 1A with AIM 9L Sidewinders and underfuselage gunpack fitted

Light-grey Hawk T.1 over the English countryside

145.

Red Arrows

Those students streamed for multi-engine pilot training and the navigational instruction course come under the auspices of No. 3 FTS at RAF Cranwell, for instruction on No. 45(R) Squadrons BAe Jetstreams and Dominie T.2s of No. 55(R) Squadron respectively. While prospective rotary-winged pilots go to the DHFS (Defence Helicopter Flying School) at RAF Shawbury, Shropshire. Apart from No. 60 Squadron with nine Agusta Bell AB 412 Griffin HT 1, with three detached to the SARTU at Valley, the DHFS operates 26 Eurocopter AS 350BA Squirrel HT 1s from Shawbury on basic and advanced single-engine helicopter flying training courses. The basic content is the premise of No. 660 Squadron AAC while No 705 Naval Air Squadron, Fleet Air Arm, RN is responsible for advanced flying. All RAF students pass through these units.

A Griffin HT 1
(Bell 412) from the SAR Training
Unit from RAF Valley, Anglesey.

Gloss-black and yellow Eurocopter AS 350 Twin Squirrel of DHFS at RAF Shawbury, Shropshire

Unofficial Badge

BAe Jetstream T1 of No. 45 Squadron base at RAF Cranwell for multi-engined type flying training

Unofficial Badge

HS Dominie (125-100) T.1 used by the RAF since the late 1960s for navigator training oridinally with No. 1 Air Navigation School at RAF Stradishall, Suffolk until unit absorbed by No. 6 FTS

Upgraded Domanie T.2 in 'new' colour scheme gloss black with white upper fuselage and wing surfaces

148.

Conventional FTS coloured Tucano. Note station badge on the tail

Gloss black Shorts Tucano T.1 turboprop trainer

149.

Miscellaneous Flying Units.
No. 17 Squadron

BAE Systems Warton Aerodrome, **Eurofighter OEU**
& SPIT (Service Pilot Instructor Training)
Eurofighter Typhoon
Motto: *Excellere contende* - Strive to excel'
Nickname: 'Black Knights'

Originally formed at Gosport on 1 February, 1915, No. 17 Squadron saw action in the Middle East during World War I and provided support to the campaign in Salonika. Later at Alexandria and Heliopolis. On its return to the UK the squadron was based at Kenley and operated as a fighter unit with Bristol Bulldog and Gloster Gauntlet biplane fighters during the 1930s. After taking part in the Battle of Britain with its Hawker Hurricanes it left for India seeing operations in Burma with the Hurricane and Spitfire. Post-war it flew briefly on target-tug duties with Bristol Beaufighter TT. 10 before moving to RAF Germany in the photo-recce role with EE Canberra PR 7. On relinquishing its Canberras in December 1969, the following year it found a new role as a MDC Phantom II strike fighter unit, transistioning to the Sepecat Jaguar in September 1975. Ten years later these were supplanted by Panavia Tornado GR 1 when No. 17 Squadron became the second of RAF Bruggens Jaguar squadrons to convert to the Tornado on 1 March, 1985. The squadron was the only user of the Paveway II LGB and provided crews for the Muharraq detachment during the Gulf War.

Under the Labour Governments SDR 1998 (Strategic Defence Review) and the imminent closure of RAF Bruggen and disbandment of the Bruggen Wing, No. 17 Squadron disbanded on 31 March, 1999. This of course involved the withdrawal from use of its twelve Tornado G.R.1 aircraft. With the first RAF Eurofighter due for handover by the end of 2002, the Warton-based OEU and SPIT, is to carry the No. 17 Squadron number-plate and will train 16 pilots on type, six for the OEU and ten for the OCU - No. 29 Squadron. Initial deliveries will be two-seaters with software cleared for the training role. The squadron (OEU) is scheduled to fly around 1,300 hours at Warton before transferring to Coningsby, to join No. 29 Squadron at the Lincolnshire base. The SPIT course will comprise two weeks ground school and four weeks flying, to include conversion to type and weapon system familiarity training. Each pilot will fly 12 sorties and around 15 hours simulator training. Night flying and in-flight refuelling will also be part of the course and qualified pilots will have completed day and night solo flights and be certified aircraft rear-seat captains.

The OEU tasking will include 790 hours flying to include four-ship formation operational mission profiles to fully evaluate the airplanes flight envelope and weapon system. This will also include a full test and evaluation of the cockpit displays and Captor radar. One of the squadrons thirteen Eurofighters will be dedicated to ground-crew training. Sixty RAF engineers will work alongside BAe personnel to obtain qualifications to maintain the airplane at Coningsby and provide instructors for future maintenance staff. Although the purpose of basing the OEU initially, at Warton is to 'derisk' the airplanes service entry, No. 17 Squadron will be an autonomous unit with its own dedicated hardstanding and unit personnel will occupy purpose-built buildings and accommodation.

Aircraft markings and codes

It is believed no unit markings were carried by No. 17 Squadrons airplanes in WW I. following disbandment in 1919, the squadron reformed in 1924, and adopted a double zigzag painted in black along the length of the fuselage and across the span of the upper mainplane of their Sopwith Snipe, Hawker Woodcock, Gloster Gamecock, A. W. Siskin, Bristol Bulldog and Gloster Gauntlet biplanes, the latter having the top decking of its fuselage painted black. After the Munich Crisis of 1938, the Gauntlets were camouflaged and carried the official code UV- on the fuselage forward of the roundel with an individual airplane letter aft. In September 1939, the official code changed to YB- which was retained throughout the war.

Post-war the squadron carried the official code UT- with most airplanes displaying its individual number painted forward of the fuselage roundel. On receiving EE Canberra PR 7s the black zigzag re-appeared on a white disc on the fin, and on the nose on each side of the squadron badge. MDC Phantoms carried the same basic markings but in the form of a broad arrowhead on the engine air intakes with the roundel superimposed. The airplanes 'last three' was painted in white on the fin. Sepecat Jaguars reverted to the rectangular markings painted on the engine air intakes on each side of a diagonally divided black and white shield which enclosed a red gauntlet. The squadron's Panavia Tornados wore an adaption of the unit's official gauntlet badge on the tail-fin, with black and white zigzags in an arrowhead on the nose with the roundel superimposed. A two-letter code, beginning with the letter C in the range 'CA' to 'CZ', appeared in red outlined in white on the fin. The unit's Eurofighter markings as yet, are undefined.

The RAF's first duel-seat Eurofighter Typhoon rolls out at BAe Systems, Warton aerodrome   (BAe)
Note: duel markings, four national roundel and low-viz RAF markings

Initial deliveries (Tranche 1) of the BAe/Ferranti Captor will be a highly capable mechanical-scan radar. Tranche 2 assemblies will embody electronic scanning, an updated CPU (Central Processor Unit) to cure obsolescence and provide growth potential as well as a re-configurable signal processor in place of the specific mission configured microprocessors. This will enhance both the air-to-air and air-to-ground modes, with adaptive beam forming and interleaving, which in turn will increase target data update rates and allow the radar to be used as a datalink and for some electronic warfare task.

Captor radar

Miscellaneous Flying Units   Air Warfare Centre F. 3 Tornado OEU. RAF Coningsby, Lincs
                                        Panavia Tornado F. 3
                                        Empire Test Pilots School Boscombe Down, Wilts
                                        Representative: Panavia F. 2 (ZD935), BAe Hawk T. 1 (XX343 '3')

Air Warfare Centre Panavia Tornado F. 3

OEU Tornado F.2
with underfuselage
instrumentation pods
fitted

Hawk T.1 '3' of
the trio operated
by the ETPS
Boscombe Down

The **Strike Attack OEU** is located at Boscombe Down, Wilts
(to re-locate to RAF Coningsby, Lincolnshire
Inventory: MDC/BAe Harrier GR 7, Panavia Tornado GR1/4
Sepecat Jaguar GR 3A

Air Warfare Centre F.3 Tornado OEU RAF Coningsby, Lincs
Panavia Tornado F.3 (to be absorbed into SAOEU
Empire Test Pilots School Boscombe Down, Wilts
Representative: Panavia F.2 (ZD935), BAe Hawk T.1 (XX343'3')

Panavia Tornado GR 4 of the Strike Attack OEU

OEU BAe Harrier GR 5

Upgraded heavily armed unmarked Sepecat Jaguar GR 3

Battle of Britain Memorial Flight Douglas Dakota PA947 used for pilots to gain tail-dragger experience and handling before flying the Lancaster B.1 PA474. The Dakota is also used to carry spares and support crews on to airshows involving a stop-over

Ex– SAAF C-47 Dakota 'Rudolph' with invasion stripes donated to BBMF

BoBMF Hawker Hurrican IIC PZ865 and Supermarine Spitfire XIX PM631

157.

BoBMF Avro Lancaster B.1 'City of Lincoln' WS-, the famous wartime code of No. 9 (Bomber) Squadron

Avro Lancaster B.1 carrying No. 103 Squadron wartime code PM-

Hawker Hurricane IIC PZ 865

Douglas Dakota C.III TS423 ex-USAAF 42-100884

RAF Northholt, Station Flight
ISLANDER BN-2T. 10 seat light utility aircraft
RAF BN-2T Islander designations CC2 (1) CC2A (1)

160.

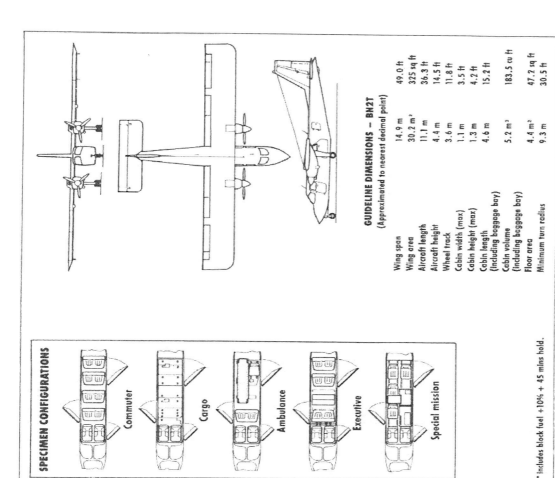

SPECIMEN CONFIGURATIONS

Commuter

Cargo

Ambulance

Executive

Special mission

Powerplant:

2 x Allison 250-B17C Turboprops rated at 320shp/238.5kW for take-off

PERFORMANCE	BN2T
Take off distance ground roll to clear 50ft (15m)	837ft/255m 1250ft/381m
Rate of climb twin engine one engine	1050ft per min 215ft per min
Absolute ceiling twin engine one engine	25000ft+/7620m+ 10000ft/3048m
Max cruise speed Economical cruise	170kt/315kph (TAS) 150kt/278kph (TAS) @ 10000ft
Stall speeds (IAS) flaps up, power off flaps down, power off	52kt/96kph 45kt/83kph
Landing distance ground roll to clear 50ft (15m)	747ft/228m 1110ft/338m
Range IFR * VFR	590nm/1093km 728nm/1349km

WEIGHTS	tip tanks standard
Max take off	7000lb/3175kg
Max landing	6800lb/3084kg
Max zero fuel	6600lb/2994kg
Payload with max fuel	1520lb/689kg
Disposable load	2960lb/1343kg
Usable fuel	215 US gal/814 ltr

Data shown here is correct for maximum weight and ISA conditions at sea level unless otherwise stated.

GUIDELINE DIMENSIONS – BN2T
(Approximated to nearest decimal point)

Wing span	14.9 m	49.0 ft
Wing area	30.2 m²	325 sq ft
Aircraft length	11.1 m	36.3 ft
Aircraft height	4.4 m	14.5 ft
Wheel track	3.6 m	11.8 ft
Cabin width (max)	1.1 m	3.5 ft
Cabin height (max)	1.3 m	4.2 ft
Cabin length (including baggage bay)	4.6 m	15.2 ft
Cabin volume (including baggage bay)	5.2 m³	183.5 cu ft
Floor area	4.4 m²	47.2 sq ft
Minimum turn radius	9.3 m	30.5 ft

* Includes block fuel +10% + 45 mins hold.

Pilatus Britten-Norman Ltd
BEMBRIDGE Isle of Wight
United Kingdom PO355PR
Tel: 0983 - 872511
Telex: 86686 / 86277
Fax: 0983 - 873246

PILATUS
BRITTEN-NORMAN

BN2T – GUIDELINE DATA

Miscellaneous Flying Units

Hunting Aviation operates a handful (5-6) Shorts SC 3 Skycan for para-training. Aircraft are civil registered

FRA operate nine Dassault Falcon 20 on Electronic Warfare (EW) training duties
Six are based at Newcastle Tyne Tees Airport, the other three are Hurn, Bournemouth

RAF Logistics Command was disbanded in November 1999, when the three separate Service (Army, Navy and Air Force) logistical organisations were merged into a single Defence Logistics Organisation formed in April 2000. Logistics Command took over part of Support Command's task when it was established at RAF Brampton and RAF Wyton in 1994. The logistics organisation has a number of specific areas it is responsible for :

1. Support management, including all logistics, storage, distribution and disposal of equipment.
2. All repair, overhaul, maintenance and modification programmes at third and fourth line level.
3. Provision and management of all communications and information systems.
4. Catering
5. Financial management and accounting for all expenditure within the organisation.

Maintenance functions includes aero-engineering, signals and movements. Responsibilities include scheduled major maintenance usually undertaken at RAF St Athan, the largest MU in the RAF, jointly manned by service and civilian personnel it can handle up to 58 aircraft at any one time. The organisation is also responsible to ensure continuous efforts are made to improve maintenance facilities, introduce new tools and better working methods to improve efficiency and reduce costs.

Logistics also has responsibility for the Repair and Salvage Squadron, which itself is responsible for salvaging all service fixed wing airplanes in all parts of the world and also carries out aircraft recovery for the Department of Transport. In addition the Repair and Salvage Squadron sends teams of tradesmen to operational stations to undertake aircraft modifications and repairs which are beyond the remit of normal station personnel, but does not require the airplane to be returned to a maintenance unit. The squadron also has responsibility for aircraft battle damage repair associated with front-line operations.

Other areas of responsibility include No. 30 MU at RAF Sealand, near Chester, which is the main avionics and instrument equipment service centre. Repairing, servicing, and testing more than 100,000 items of airborne radio, radar, electrical, instrument and missile equipment a year. In addition the unit is responsible for the periodic calibration of all test equipment, as well as the manufacture of specific test equipment, and interconnect cables as required.

The RAF Armament Support Unit (RAFASUPU) is based at the home of the Harrier at Wittering and is home to the RAF Explosive Ordnance Disposal (EOD) Squadron which is responsible for all training and trials associated with special weapons and ordnance etc. A small headquarters team also ensures all Health and Safety Regulations are adhered to. In addition to all major aero-engineering tasks, the organisation repairs and maintains almost any kind of equipment in service use, such as parachutes, ground equipment, furniture and domestic equipment. A number of large workshops at each Equipment Supply Depot undertakes the repair and servicing of almost any item of equipment on its inventory.

The Defence Logistics Organisation is responsible for all MU scheduled routine maintenance, including engines and armaments

There are seven signals units with responsibility for the support of all aspects of telecommunication, ground radio and signals engineering. These comprised in four main categories. First, a large complex of HF (High Frequency) transmitters and receivers in the UK including communications centres with automatic message routine equipment. Second, all message relay centres both automatic and manual and also manages the General Purpose Telephone Network as well as all secure systems ensuring the correct procedures are adhered to. Third, it operates the Skynet Satellite Communications System, offering overseas communications, in telegraphed, data and speech format, as well as a management service for the NATO 4 series of satellites. Finally, repairs all ground radio and radar equipments, radio navigation aids and beacons and point-to-point and ground-to-air communication. This embraces an antenna maintenance service world-wide, all training of personnel for these tasks being undertaken at the Aerial Erector School at RAF Digby, Lincs.

Also included are responsibilities for all electrical engineering associated with the entire field of communications equipment, air traffic control and defence radar systems and ground-based navigation aids. This includes undertaking feasibility studies, project management, design, development etc., involving a large team of engineers and technicians, design staff, and draughtsmen.

A Lockheed Tristar undergoing hanger maintenance

Looking to the Future.

With the Eurofighter set to replace the Tornado ADV F. 3s within the decade, and its multi-role development likely to replace the Sepecat Jaguars at Coltishall, and sixty Lockheed Martin F-35 to re-equip the Joint Harrier Strike force at RAF Cottesmore. Ninety F-35s are likely to replace the bulk of the 144 Panavia Tornado GR 4s. Whether the air force will commission another manned fixed wing strike plane remains to be seen. A possible manned GR 4 replacement is shown below.

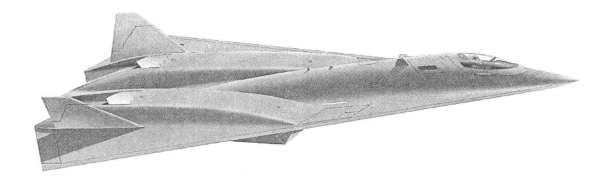

However, there is a possibility that the GR 4 Tornado will be the last front-line manned overland attack strike plane as operations in Afghanistan with UCAVs has proved beyond any doubt this is where the future lies for the modern air force. New advances in computer power and remote control techniques promise a bright future for these aircraft in war and peace. In June 1997, a pilotless remote-controlled aircraft powered entirely by solar energy, flew to a height of 67,000 feet over Hawaii. Its surface area being almost entirely, wing, it remained aloft for 13 hours 39 minutes, the power for its eight small propellers coming from its wing-mounted solar panels. In August 1998 a joint US-Australian project team with its "Aerosonde" UAV became the first unmanned aircraft to fly the Atlantic. With a wing-span of less than three metres, it used satellite navigation and consumed just six litres of fuel to make the 2,000-mile crossing from Newfoundland to the Outer Hebrides. The object of the flight was to demonstrate the feasibility of using UAVs to collect weather information and relay it back to the weathermen, civil and military.

For many years, the USAF had a very effective UAV, the Teledyne Ryan AGM-34, that was even used in Vietnam being either ground or air-launched. But since 1982, it is the Israelis who have lead the way,with the effective use of UAVs in the Bekaa Valley in the Middle East,and even earlier in the 1973 Arab-Israeli War. With the design and development of small remotely-controlled aircraft, especially as battlefield surveillance vehicles to relay essential recconniassance data back to their artillery or air force command centres. Similar UAVs have recently entered service with the British and US forces. The US Global Hawk was used in Kosovo to good effect, although not without a number of losses to Serb SAMs. Suddenly, UAVs have become the future for the military, not only in the battlefield surveillance role, but also as high-altitude spy planes and as future combat aircraft. The RAF has already indicated that its Tornado GR 4 replacement could well be an unmanned strike aircraft.

In the United States, future unmanned VTOL aircraft and strike bombers to operate from large floating aerodromes are being evaluated. Serious studies into the use of UAVs by the US military started in 1979, with the Aquila Programme. It was planned to build some 780 surveillance aircraft for use by the US Army at a cost of $563 million. It was planned that the prop-driven Aquila should be small enough to be carried by four infantrymen, using real-time video and infra-red for day/night operation. However by 1987, the project was 200% over-budget with an estimated further $1 billion needed to buy less than half the aircraft originally planned. Difficulties arose in making the system resistant to enemy electronic countermeasures. Of over 100 trial flights the equipment failed to work properly excepting for only seven times. As a consequence the project was abandoned.

Another failed US UAV project was the US Navys "Pioneer" programme, an attempt to develop a pilotless spotter plane for launch from battleships to assist naval gunners to plot their targets. Then rather than develop their own unmanned aircraft the Americans utilised an existing Israeli design, acquiring seventy-two aircraft and nine remote-control systems, for less than $90 million. Initial US shore-based tests with Pioneer proved satisfactory although problems arose when Pioneer went to sea. The main problems were with the recovery system, a method of grabbing in a net which lead to much damage to the vehicle. A similar recovery problem has dogged the latest British UAV, with its inverted balloon cushioning landing gear which has been so problematic. The American Pioneer also suffered a series of mysterious crashes which was eventually traced to the warships on-board electronics interfering with the UAVs guidance systems. However, since the problems were resolved, Pioneer has been used very successfully operationally in the Gulf, Somalia, and the Balkan conflicts. In the Gulf War six Pioneer UAV units were deployed, two on Navy battleships, three US Marine Corps companies and a US Army Platoon. In total almost fifty Pioneers flew more than 530 sorties amounting to nearly 1,700 combat hours. Performing a variety of missions over both land and sea, at least one Pioneer UAV was airborne throughout the duration of the war with reportedly only one lost to enemy fire! Certainly this was not the case in the Kosovo Crisis, where a number of UAVs were lost to enemy fire, with three Canadair/Dornier CL-289 surveillance craft lost in one week, resulting in the suspension of all further flights. In addition to recce and surveillance missions, UAVs are ideal vehicles for numerous other tasks, including aerial decoys.

In August 1998, at the insistence of the US Navy work started on development of an American VTOL UAV; as the "net" recovery of UAVs at sea was still proving less than satisfactory. A number of interesting VTOL machines has been produced including a scaled down V-22 Osprey from Bell/Boeing and an offering from Bombardier named the Guardian which utilises two contra-rotating sets of rotors mounted one above the other.

With Britain having stated a firm interest in an UCAV to replace its Tornado strike bombers in the next century, American aeronautical engineers are hoping to demonstrate a practical combat UAV by 2002. The aircraft is likely to be of stealth design, without a tail-fin to lessen its radar profile. With the new manoeuvrability brought about with the new computer control systems, it is likely it will be able to be equipped with a "dog-fight" mode to counter possible manned attackers. It is thought the plane would be capable of flying thousands of miles on a single mission, taking out enemy anti-aircraft sites and suppressing enemy defences, whilst remaining to protect conventional manned bombers and ground-attack aircraft that might be sent in later.

Current UAVs and those for the immediate future require a skilled operator (pilot) to operate them, either in the air from their manned fixed or rotary winged counterparts or from ground control centres.

However, at the Cranfield University, School of Aeronautics, Bedfordshire, England, considerable work is being done on 'de-skilling' the control of UAVs. The senior lecturer in flight dynamics Peter Thomasson, explained that the University had done "some clever work, where the airplane flies itself." "You just tell it where to go and what to do. You can have a picture coming back from the aircraft on a screen and you just point with your finger and it goes there and observes the point indicted." It is of interest that already with the French looking to develop its Rafale Mach 2 multi-role combat plane further in the 21st Century, it has been been considered as an airborne controller for a French UCAV. There are other fields, (other than military) where the UAV is likely to come into its own in the future, namely in hazardous situations (i.e. nuclear powerplant and natural disasters, floods etc) and also where modern superior air traffic control systems are in operation, unmanned civil airliners could be used, making air travel even safer! As most airline accidents are caused by pilot or air traffic control errors and not mechanical failures.

Predator UAV currently in operational service with the USAF. Used to good effect in Afghanistan and over Iraq in the recce/surveillance role and in Yemen on an armed attack on Al Qeada terrorists

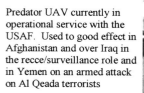

167.

Towards the end of the 21st Century there will undoubtedly be some new and unusual designs of both civil and military airplanes, but also there is no doubt that mainly due to cost, throughout the early part of the century there will be very little change, and most civil and military airplanes will be little different from the designs and shapes we are already familiar with. As shown by this mock-up of the Future Large (Transport) Aircraft.

Airbus A400M FLA
Future Large Airplane
25 ordered by RAF

Albeit, underneath the familiar facades will be a wealth of new technology, new materials, new and more efficient aero-engines, electronics (avionics) and other high technology systems, such as advanced flight management systems (FMS) with embedded Global Positioning Systems (GPS) embodying world-wide precision landing capability.

As with the past decade the most significant advances will be in the electronics field, all of which will have considerable effect on new military and civil airplane designs. Lasers, direct voice interfacing (DVI) to be included in EFA (Eurofighter), computer generated graphics, high-speed computers and artificial intelligence will be the order of the day. It should be said, as in other areas of modern life, considerable thought will need to be given as to how all these new systems with seemingly unending stream of information and capabilities are presented in a user friendly manner, to hopefully reduce the pilots workload and not as could easily happen, increase it. Instead leading to pilot (information) overload.

Having gone through a period when more modest speeds (Mach 0.9 - Mach 2.2) were the order of the day for the military, in its quest to maintain air superiority in future conflicts, the next generation combat designs will look to high speed (high Mach), stealth, and manoeuvrability (supermaneuverability - with thrust vectoring)), to increase the ability to survive, both in air-to-air combat and to evade the new threats from new more deadly SAMs (Surface-to-Air Missiles). Of great importance will be long-range, high-speed (Mach 2.4-3.2) aircraft with an effective payload and able to operate anywhere in the world. Fly-by-wire control systems and re-configurable signal processors will permit the airplane to be re-roled even whilst in flight. In addition the USAF is developing self-repairing flight-control systems (re-configuring and re-defining remaining undamaged systems in flight), which would permit a battle damaged airplane to be recovered to its home base at high speed.

By definition high speed (Mach) is a direct product of the propulsion system, which for these fifth generation airplanes it is believed could have engines with only 1,000 to 2,000 parts, as compared to the 15,000 to 20,000 parts used today. This drastic reduction in the 'part count' will be brought about by the use of new materials and advanced manufacturing techniques, permitting complex parts to be produced as single units with a minimum of machining and finishing being required. Reduction in parts and component count will naturally lead to reduced MToWs (Maximum Take-off Weights) so that engines will achieve thrust-to-weight ratios in the order of 20 : 1.

Appendix 1.   United Kingdom RAF. Royal Air Force - Battle Order

NB: JHC = Joint Helicopter Command (under Army control - H.Q. Erskine Barracks, Wilton - includes AAC Gazelles and Lynx)

SQUADRON	EQUIPMENT	BASE
No. 1 "Shiny Firsts"	Harrier GR 7/T.10	Cottesmore
No. 2	Tornado GR 4/GR 4A	Marham
No. 3	Harrier GR 7/T.10	Cottesmore
No. 4	Harrier GR 7/T.10	Cottesmore
No. 6 "Flying Tin Openers	Jaguar GR 3/GR 3A,T.2A/T4	Coltishall
No. 7 (JHC)	ChinookHC 2/ (6) HC 3 (2003) Gazelle HT	Odiham
No. 8	Boeing Sentry E-3D Sentry AEW 1	Waddington
No. 9	Tornado GR 4	Marham
No. 10 "Shiny Ten"	BAC VC 10 C1K	Brize Norton
No. 11	Tornado F. 3	Leeming
No. 12 "Flying Foxes"	Tornado GR 4	Lossiemouth
No. 13	Tornado GR 4/4A	Marham
No. 14 "Crusaders"	Tornado GR 4	Lossiemouth
No. 15(R) (TWCU)	Tornado GR 4	Lossiemouth
No. 16(R) "Saints" 226 OCU	Jaguar GR 3/3A/T 2A/T4 (*moving to Coltishall*)	Lossiemouth
No. 17(R) "Black Knights"	Eurofighter Typhoon OEU (13)	BAe Warton Aerodrome, Lancs
No. 18 (JHC)	Chinook HC 2/HC 2A	Odiham
No. 19(R) (4 FTS)	Hawk T1/T1A/T1W	Valley
No. 20(R) "Double Crossers" 233 OCU	Harrier GR 7/T.4/T.10	Wittering
No. 22 SAR "Dinky Do's"		
H.Q. & A Flt	Sea King HAR 3A	RMB Chivenor (24 hr cover)
B Flt	Sea King HAR 3A	Wattisham (AAC base)
C Flt	Sea King HAR 3A	RAF Valley, Anglesey
No. 23 STS	Sentry Training Squadron. Sentry AEW 1	Waddington
No. 24	Hercules C-130J	Lyneham
No. 25	Tornado F 3	Leeming
No. 27 & 240 OCF (JHC)	Chinook HC 2	Odiham
No. 28 (JHC)	Merlin HC. 3	Benson
No. 29(R)	Eurofighter Typhoon OCU (spring 2004)	Coningsby
No. 30	Hercules C-130J	Lyneham
No. 31	Tornado GR 4	Marham
No. 32 (Royal)	BAe 146 (2) BAe 125 CC3 Comms VIP Aerospatiale Twin Squirrel (leased)	

No. 33 (JHC)	Puma HC 1	Benson
No. 39 (1 PRU)	Canberra P.R. 9/T.4	Marham
No. 41	Jaguar GR 3/3A/T 4	Coltishall
No. 42(R) & 236 OCF	Nimrod MR 2	Kinloss
No. 43 "Fighting Cocks"	Tornado F 3	Leuchars
No. 45(R) "Flying Camels" 3 FTS	Jetstream T. 2	Cranwell
No. 47	Hercules C 1/ C 3	Lyneham
No. 51 (ELINT)	Nimrod R. 1P (E.1)	Waddington
No. 54	Jaguar GR. 3/GR. 3A/ T.2A/T.4	Coltishall
No. 55(R)	HS Dominie T 2	Cranwell
No. 56(R) "Firebirds" 229 OCU	Tornado F 3 *(to RAF Leuchars 2004)*	Coningsby
No. 57(R) 242 OCU	Hercules C 1/ C 3 *Plus C-130J C4/C5 Conversion Flight*	Lyneham
No. 60(R) DHFS	Bell Griffin HT 1 (6)	Shawbury
SAR Training Unit	Bell Griffin HT 1 (3)	Valley

Currently (2002), the planned introduction of Eurofighter Typhoon into front-line service, is for most to replace Panavia Tornado F.3 variants with their respective units and the possible re-introduction of No. 74 'Tiger' Squadron into the battleorder. In addition to the OEU (4) and OCU (24) airplanes, the RAF will maintain a 137 airplane front-line Eurofighter fleet, with 84 placed in storage as attrition replacements and used on rotation to spread airframe hours. Introduction into front-line service details:

2 x air defence units to re-equip at six month intervals at Coningsby June 2004 and 2005.
1 x air defence unit to re-equip at Leeming during mid-2006.
1 x day/night fighter-bomber unit at Leeming in mid-2007
1 x air defence unit and 2 multi-role units will form at Leuchars, between late 2007 and September 2009.
No. 1435 Flight at Mount Pleasant in the Falkland Islands will receive its four replacement airplanes in 2009.

No. 45

No. 60

SQUADRON	EQUIPMENT	BASE
No. 70	Hercules C 1/C 3	Lyneham
No. 72(R) 1 FTS	Shorts Tucano T. 1	Linton-on-Ouse
No. 78	Chinook (1), Sea King HAR 3 (2)	RAF Mount Pleasant (Falkland Islands)
Red Arrows Aerobatic Team	Hawk T.1 910)	Scampton, Lincs
No. 84	Wessex HC 2C (3) *(wfu March 2003)* *to be replaced by civil-registered Bell 412*	RAF Akrotiri (Cyprus)
No. 99	Boeing/MDC C-17 Globemaster III	Brize Norton
No. 100 "Aggressors"	Hawk T1/T 1A	Leeming
No. 101	BAC VC 10 K2/K3/K4	Brize Norton
No. 111 "Treble One"	Tornado F 3	Leuchars
No. 120	Nimrod MR 2P	Kinloss
No. 201	Nimrod MR 2P	Kinloss
No. 202 SAR		
HQ & A Flt	Sea King HAR 3	Boulmer
D Flt	Sea King HAR 3	Lossiemouth
E Flt	Sea King HAR 3	Leaconfield
No. 203(R) SKOCU	Sea King HAR 3A (3)	St Mawgan
No. 206	Nimrod MR 2P	Kinloss
No. 207(R) 1 FTS	Short Tucano	Linton-on-Ouse
No. 208(R) 4 FTS	Hawk T1/T1A	Valley
No. 216	Tristar K1/KC1/C2/C2A (9)	Brize Norton
No. 230 (JHC)	Puma HC 1	Aldergrove (Northern Ireland)
No. 617 "Dambusters"	Tornado GR4	Lossiemouth
No. 660 (AAC) DHFS	Aerospatiale Squirrel H.T. 1	Shawbury
No. 705 (FAA) DHFS	Aerospatiale Squirrel H.T. 1	Shawbury
No. 800 FAA	Sea Harrier F/A 2	Cottesmore
No. 801 FAA	Sea Harrier F/A 2	Cottesmore
No. 845 FAA (JHC)	Sea King HC 4 Commando	Yeovilton
No. 846 FAA (JHC)	Sea King HC 4 Commando	Yeovilton
No. 847 FAA (JHC)	Sea King HC 4 Commando	Yeovilton
No. 848 FAA (JHC)	Sea King HC 4 Commando	Yeovilton
No 899 FAA	Sea Harrier F/A 2 & T. 8N	Wittering

ABBREVIATIONS:

AAR	Air-to-Air Refuelling
AD	Air Defence
AEW	Airborne Early Warning
ASW	Anti-Submarine Warfare
DHFS	Defence Helicopter Flying School
ELINT	ELectronic INTelligence
FAC	Forward Air Controller
FGA	Fighter Ground Attack
Flt	Flight
FTS	Flying Training School
JHC	Joint Helicopter Command
MR	Maritime Patrol Reconnaissance
OCF	Operational Conversion Flight
OCU	Operational conversion Unit
OEU	Operational Evaluation Unit
PRU	Photographic Reconnaissance Unit
SAR	Search And Rescue
SH	Support Helicopter
SIGINT	SIGnals INTelligence
SKOCU	Sea King Operational Conversion Unit
TWCU	Tornado Weapons Conversion Unit

No. 207 SQDN.

No. 72

APPENDIX II: BASIC DATA

Airplane	Type	Engines	Wingspan	Length	Max Speed	Range	Accomodation Weapons/Remarks
Airbus A400M	Tactical Transport						
BAC VC 10 Super VC 10	Long-range tanker/transport	4 x 21,800lb s.t. R-R Conway turbofans	44.5m (146ft 2in)	52.32m including probe.	Max Cruising at 9,450m 935km/h (581 mph)	6,273 km (3,898 miles)	Flight crew of four.
BAe Hawk T.1	Trainer	1 x 5,200lb s.t. R-R/ Turbomeca Adour 151 turbofan	9.36m (30ft 9.75in)	11.17m (36ft 7.75in)	990 km/h (615 mph)	998 km (620 miles)	Two crew. T.1 can carry up to 3.084kg 6,800-lb
BAe Hawk 100	LIFT	1 x 5,845lb s.t. R-R/ Turbomeca Adour 871 turbofan	9.39m (30ft 10in)	11.68m (38ft 4 in)	1,038 km/h (645 mph)	combat radius 510 km (317 miles)	Optional 30mm Aden cannon 3,000kg (6,614 lb) 2x AIM 9L
BAe Jetstream	Multi-engine trainer	2 x 996ehp Turbomeca Astazou XVID turboprops	15.85m (52ft 0in)	14.37m (47ft 1.5in)	454 km/h (282 mph)	2,224 km (1,380 miles)	Pilot & Trainee Plus four
BAe Dominie (125-700B)	Navigation Trainer	2 x 3,700lb s.t. Garrett TFE 731-3-1RH turbofans	14.33m (47ft 0in)	15.46m (50ft 8.5in)	808km/h cruise (502 mph)	4,482 km (2,785 miles)	up to 14 passengers plus crew
BAe 146-100	VIP/ VVIP	4 x 6,970lb s.t. Avco Lycoming ALF 502R-5 turbofans	26.34m (86ft 5in)	26.2m (85ft 11.5in)	709 km/h cruise (440 mph)	1,733 km (1,077 miles) with max payload	Twenty VIP passengers Plus crew
BAe Nimrod MR 2	Maritime Recce ELINT	4 x 12,140ib s.t. R-R RB.168-20 Spey turbofans	35.00m (114ft 10in)	38.63m (126ft 9 in)	787 km/h cruise (490 mph)	12 hours endurance max 15 hours	Twelve crew 9 torpedos, bombs, 2 x AIM 9L Harpoon anti-ship missiles rockets/mines
Boeing Vertol Chinook	Medium lift helicopter	2 x 3,000 shp Textron Lycoming T-55-L-712 turboshafts	18.29m (60ft 0in) rotor (each)	15.54m (51ft 0in)	291 km/h (181 mph)	185km (115 miles) radius	Two crew plus 44 troops 24 stretchers 12,000 kg (28,000lb) load
Boeing C-17 Globemaster III	Long-range heavy transport	4 x P &W 41,700 lb s.t. F117-P-100 turbofans	50.29m (165 ft 0in) (9 ft winglets)	53.04m (174ft 0in)	463 km/h (288 mph)	925 km (575 miles) with 36,786kg (81,100lb) load	Crew plus 202 personnel or 18 pallets
Boeing E-3D Sentry	AEW and Control plane	4 x 24,000lb s.t. CFM56 turbofans	44.42m (145ft 9in)	46.61m (152ft 11in)	853km/h (530 mph)	1,612km (1,002 miles) for 6 hr patrol max end. 11 hrs	
Bombardier Global Express	ASTOR Battlefield Control Plane						
Eurocopter Twin Squirrel							

Airplane	Type	Engines	Wingspan	Length	Max Speed	Range	Accomodation Weapons/Remarks
EE Canberra PR 9	High-altitude Photo-recce	2 x 7,400lb s.t. R-R Avon 109 turbojets	19.51m (63ft 11.5in)	19.96 (65ft 6in)	871 km/h (541 mph)	5,842 km (3,630 miles)	Two crew
Eurofighter Typhoon	Multi-role fighter	2 x 20,250lb s.t. Eurojet EJ200 afterburning turbofans	10.95m (34ft 5.5in)	15.96m (47ft 7in)	2,125km/h (1,321 mph) Mach 2	Combat radius 463 to 556km (288 and 345 miles)	Pilot 13 Hard Points for weapons tanks & stores
EHI 101 Merlin							
Lockheed Tri-star K. 1	Tanker Transport	3 x 50,000lb s.t. R-R RB211-524B turbofans	47.34m (155ft 4 in)	50.05m (164ft 2.5 in)			Total fuel capacity 136,080 kg (300,000 lb)
Lockheed Hercules C-130	Tactical Transport	4 x 4,508ehp Allison T56-A-15 turboprops	40.41m (132ft 7 in)	29.79m (97ft 9 in)	595km/h (370 mph)	3,791 km (2,356 miles)	Crew 4/5 92 troops 64 paratroops 74 stretchers 19,686 kg
Lockheed Hercules C-130J	Tactical Transport	4 x Allison 2100 turboprops					
Lockheed Martin F-35							
MDC/BAE Harrier GR 7	STOVL Close Support fighter	1 x R-R 21,750lb s.t. Pegasus Mk 105 turbofan	9.25m (30 ft 4 in)	14.36m (47 ft 1.5 in)	967 km/h (601 mph)	889 km (553 miles)	2 x 25-mm cannon (not used). Ordnance 4,173 kg (9,200 lb) SNEB, CRV-7 CBU-87. AIM-9L etc.
T Mk 10	Combat Capable trainer						
BAe Sea Harrier F/A 2	Shipborne STOVL fighter	1 x R-R 21,500lb s.t. Pegasus Mk 106 turbofan	7.70m (25 ft 3 in)	14.50m (47 ft 4 in)	1,185 km/h (736 mph)	Combat Radius 750km (460 miles)	2 x 30mm cannon pods 4 x AMRAAM ALARM Sea Eagle etc
Panavia Tornado IDS	Interdictor Strike	2 x 16,075lb s.t. Turbo-Union RB.199 103 turbofans	13.91m spread (45 ft 7.25 in) 8.60m swept (28 ft 2.5 in)	16.72m (54 ft 10.25in)	1,482 km/h (921 mph)	Combat radius 1,390km (863 miles)	2 x 27mm gun Ordnance 9,000 kg (19,841 lb) bombs & LGBs
Panavia Tornado ADV	Long-range Interceptor	2 x 16,520lb s.t. Turbo-Union RB. 199 104 turbofans	As for IDS	18.68m (61 ft 3.5 in)	2,338 km/h (1,453 mph) Mach 2.2	Endurance 2 hr CAP 740km (460 miles)	1 x 27mm gun 4 x Skyflash 4 x AIM 9L AMRAAM ASRAAM etc
Sepecat Jaguar	Single-seat Strike fighter	2 x Adour Mk 104 turbofans	8.69m (28 ft 6 in)	16.83m (55 ft 2.5 in)	1,699 km/h (1,056 mph) Mach 1.6	852km (530 miles) radius	Pilot. 2 x 30mm guns Ordnance 4,536 kg (10,000 lb) AAMs etc
Shorts Tucano	Trainer						
Westland Puma HC 1	Medium transport Assault helicopter	2 x 1,575 shp Turbomeca Turmo IVC turboshafts	15.00m (49 ft 2.6 in) main rotor	14.06m (46 ft 1.5 in)	262 km/h (163 mph) max cruise at sea level	550 km (342 miles) Operational range	Payload 3,000 kg (6,614 lb)
Westland Sea King HAR 3/3A	SAR/ASW multi-role Helicopter	2 x 1,660 shp R-R Gnome H.1400-1 turboshafts	18.90m (62 ft 0 in) main rotor	17.02m (55 ft 10 in)	240 km/h 126 mph	1,230 km (765 miles) Operational range	Payload 2,722 kg (6,000 lb)

APPENDIX III: National Markings (introduction of)

It was the French that first introduced national markings on military airplanes, in 1912, with the adaption of the Tricolour in a roundel which is still used to this day. At this time neither the British or the Germans saw any need for national markings but it was not to be long before the need to identify friend or foe in the heat of battle, came to the fore. The Germans lead the way with the introduction of the Black Iron Cross on 28 September 1914, when Lt Osmond RNAS, observed a German aeroplane so marked from his armoured car.

By this time as some British pilots had already experienced the unpleasantness of being fired on by their own infantry, a number of British crews had already painted a Union Jack on their aircraft under the wings. With others not only on the wings, but on the rudder, fin and fuselage sides as in addition to friendly fire British pilots who were forced to land even if on friendly territory were often treated with suspicion or hostility by the French ! Thus the first national markings carried on British aircraft were actually carried to protect them from their Allies ! However, by 26 October 1914, the Admiralty ordered that all RNAS aircraft should carry Union Jack markings on the underside of the wings. In deference to the fact that the RFC had already found the marking impracticable, as it had already been realised a "shape" is more easily discerned at a distance than colours, and that the central Red Cross of St George that forms the basis of the Union Jack could under certain conditions, at a distance, be easily confused with the German Iron Cross. It was not long before the RNAS themselves realised this and both services made their own representations as to how the problem might be overcome. So it was by the end of 1914, two different forms of national markings appeared in use on British military aircraft in the field. GHQ decreed, RFC aircraft should, from 11 December 1914, carry a roundel, similar to the French roundel, but with the colour order reversed. On 17 December the Admiralty issued instructions that all RNAS aircraft should carry a red ring with a white centre on their wings. And for a time the Union Jack was officially retained on the fuselage sides and rudder assemblies. But some RNAS pilots also marked Union Jacks under the wings in addition to the roundels. In fear the significance of the roundel was not understood.

The first aircraft of both services to bear new national markings were the bombers. In the RFC these were primarily reconnaissance types, that were occasionally used for bomb-dropping, and Sopwith Tabloids used for scouting. In the RNAS the first types to carry the official Admiralty new red ring marking were the Short Seaplanes of the Harwich Force, assigned to the airplane carriers *Engadine* (serials 119 and 120), *Riviera* (serials 135, 136 and 811), *Empress* (serials 812, 814 and 815). To avoid confusion by 1915, the national markings were modified and standardised. In May 1915, the RFC had introduced "rudder striping" in Union Jack colours, with the blue stripe in front at the rudder post, then white, and then red. It was stated that from this time Union Jacks displayed on fins and fuselage sides were no longer appropriate. In June, the RFC declared all aircraft should carry coloured roundels on fuselage sides and wings, and by late June all RFC aircraft on the Western Front were thus marked.

Unfortunately this was not the end of the matter, as having assimilated the idea of roundels from the French, with the same red, white and blue colours these themselves lead to confusion, which was not finally sorted out until 1930 ! The confusion was compounded by the RNAS original red ring markings, and that at times aircraft accepted by Britain from French manufacturers were left with their French roundels emblazoned. When it was pointed out to the users that the roundel colours were in the wrong order, they were simply painted over in the correct order but in the same original proportions which of course meant they were still incorrect..!

In addition further confusion occurred in WW II when it was decided all active flying units including training and conversion units and University Air Squadrons etc., should carry official unit code lettering to indicate which squadron they were from. As an example a Hurricane F.I marked AL-could be a No.79 or No. 429 (RCAF) Squadron airplane, both units allocated AL-. Albeit, for those in the know ,the Hurricane was a No. 79 Squadron airplane as No.429 Squadron aircraft carrying the same code were H.P. Halifax or Avro Lancaster bombers.

The protracted introduction and standardisation of national markings — outlined in chronological order.

1914

22 October	The Royal Aircraft Factory at Farnborough, issued a report on visibility of Union Jacks as displayed on aircraft following experiments with B.E.2a serial 201 on 19 October 1914.
26 October	The RNAS issued instructions that aircraft should carry Union Jacks on the underside of the lower wing.
11 December	Roundels to be marked on RFC aircraft, under wings.
17 December	Red ring with white centre used by RNAS until November 1915.

1915

16 May	Rudder striping was introduced, with blue at rudder post, white in middle, then blue. On all British aircraft.
23 June	Roundels to be displayed on fuselage sides and upper surface of top wings.
1 November	RNAS stopped using red/white ring markings. Aircraft to carry same roundel markings as RFC aircraft. Standardised roundel to be, in proportion 5:3:1 with blue outer, white middle and red inner.

1916

12 September	Officially white circle to be displayed on night flying aircraft, mainly bombers. In reality was very rarely used.

1917

18 August	Official orders were issued with regard to standardisation of aircraft markings on Western Front, and the requirement for the gradual removal of all unauthorised embellishments.
23 December	Further changes to markings of units deployed on the Western Front.

1918

3 January	Low-viz dull blue, dull red, roundel recommended for night bombers (minus white inner circle) Introduced November 1918, retained until 1937.
6 August	First steps to introduce low-viz night roundel as above.

1930

15 July	Finally to avoid confusion with French aircraft, R.A.F. is notified rudder stripe colouring to be reversed, i.e. red leading at rudder post with blue trailing.
29 September	All contractors, manufacturers, instructed to implement rudder striping change on all aircraft delivered or re-delivered from this date.
31 October	Order issued rudder striping changes must be implemented, with immediate effect.

1934

1 August	Rudder striping discontinued, and roundel size reduced so as to ensure the markings do not spill over onto ailerons, and control surfaces.

Aircraft Numbering

In parallel with the introduction of national and squadron markings, it was also realised that a system of identification of airframes for record identification purposes was needed. The current letter/ number system used by Britain for its military aircraft can be traced back almost 85 years.

With the deployment of airplanes in 1912, both the Navy and the Army were serialising the aircraft they received independently. However, for records and tracing purposes confusion was already arising, particularly when similarly numbered airplanes from the two services were brought together on joint exercises and operations. In the realisation that this duplication would soon lead to great confusion, the two services agreed to a degree of standardisation for procurement purposes. The system was uncomplicated and extremely simple starting logically as one would expect at No.1 continuing on numerically. However, to take into account airframes already delivered and cover future deliveries, initial number allocations were split between the Admiralty and Army as follows.

Nos.	1 to 200	Admiralty.	Circa	1912
Nos.	201 to 800	Army		1912
Nos.	801 to 1600	Admiralty		1914
Nos.	1601 to 3000	Army		1914
Nos.	3001 to 4000	Admiralty		1915
Nos.	4001 to 8000	Army		1916
Nos.	8001 to 10000	Admiralty		1916

In 1916, it was realised that with the proliferation in aircraft available to the military and increasing all the time that a new system was needed so as not to create continually lengthy and unwieldy numbers and it was decided to start the sequence again, at '1' but this time prefixed with a letter. This was the start of the system still in use today. The Army were allocated from A1 onwards and the Admiralty from N1 on. The Army proceeded through its allocation as new airframes were registered and by April 1918 coincident with the formation of the RAF it had reached the letter E.

The first problem with the system arose when allocating the C prefix. The problem occurred due to the fact that Flying Training Units in Canada who had been procuring Curtiss JN-4 'Jenny' locally had been serialising them in the C101 to C2500 sequence 'C', standing for Canada. Quite unwittingly therefore duplication of the serial had occurred after only five years. However, the RAF continued with the system after having decided not to use a number of letters due to the possibility of confusion with other letters or numerals. The decision not to use I , M (already in use for ground training airframes), O, Q, U or Y reduced the system to a 20 letter alphabet.

By the end of WW I allocations had reached J. Cessation of activities naturally slowing new aircraft deliveries considerably, meant of course the rapid conservation of letter allocations was also achieved.

By the late 1920s, allocations were being made in the 'K' sequence. It was at this time it was decided to make a minor but significant change to the system by declaring that in order to standardise on a 5 digit serial that from L on, the numeral sequence would start at 1000 (L1000) instead of 1. This is the system still used today. Another small but strategically important change introduced at this time (and again, still used today), was that "gaps" were intentionally left in the sequential allocations intended as a deliberate attempt to disguise the true number of aircraft in existence. These unused numbers were known as "Blackout Blocks". As previously mentioned M was not used and N had been set aside for naval allocations. Surprisingly, duplication again occurred when N was used for RAF aircraft as a follow -on to L. O was not used so P became the follow on to N. P, included large blocks of Supermarine Spitfire and Hawker Hurricane allocations. Q was not used and the sequence followed on logically to R. With the declaration of WW II the volume of orders increased with S to follow on.

However, by 1925, the Navy had used all its 'N' allocation and subsequently started to utilise the S prefix. It was decided therefore to leave S dedicated to Naval types and jump to T. The T prefix contained the first impressed civilian aircraft and also contained large blocks of training aircraft, urgent requirements of course existing for training new aircrews and obviously reflecting the large expansion in pilot training at the time. U was not used the numbering sequence continuing to V. More impressed aircraft were in the V sequence and two consecutive batches of Hawker Hurricanes were allocated (V6533 - 7195) & (V7200 - 8127) a total of 1,191 airframes. V was followed logically by the W sequence which registration W4041 was given to Britains first jet the "Weaver" E.28/39 Gloster's single-engined experimental predecessor, with the Whittle engine, to the twin-engined Gloster Meteor F.1. As new airframes deliveries gathered apace with X and Z (Y not used) prefixes used within a year of hostilities breaking out.

With all Alpha prefixes having been allocated, what was to do! Fortunately the most logical path was selected and three numerics were preceded by two letters thus maintaining the five digit serial. Starting at AA100 (a Bristol Blenheim). Again, certain letter sequences were not used, to avoid confusion.

C was not used as it could be confused with G. But G was used as there was no C. M was brought back into use with the "double letter" system. While again I, O, Q, U, and Y were not used. Establishing the 20 letter alphabet in use today. Also a number of double letter combinations were NOT USED for various reasons as detailed in table below.

AC   Not used. As commonly used abbreviation for "aircraft".
DA100 to DD599   Not used. Had been allocated to British Purchasing Commission to the United States.
                 (orders were cancelled abruptly with the introduction of Lend-Lease) DD600 onwards were used.
DH   Not used. As was used as common abbreviation for "de Havilland".
EA   Not used. A common abbreviation for "Enemy aircraft."
HA   Not used.   Commonly used to annotate "Hostile aircraft"
HT   Not used.   Commonly applied/used as "High Tension" - HT in electrical circuits.
JE
JH
JJ
KR to KT. Lend-Lease allocation - Not used.
MR.   Commonly used for abbreviated aircraft "role" allocation. MR - Maritime Patrol aircraft.
SA to SK   Lend-Lease allocation - Not used.
SV   Commonly used in abbreviation ASV for "Surface Vessel" (ship).
TN   Cancelled orders
TR
NZ   Prefix for New Zealand
VE   "Victory in Europe".

An anomaly occurred in the double-letter sequence when the prefix NC was used (NC414-) allocated to a batch of Vickers Wellington XIV bombers. A mistake, perhaps..! A similar mistake occurred in 1973, when prefixes XY101-120 were assigned to part of a Sepecat Jaguar order. Also XY125 was allocated to a USMC Harrier that was being used as a demonstrator aboard a French helicopter carrier. This drew attention to the error, and subsequently all Jaguar "XY" allocations were changed to XZ before the aircraft were built. By 1945, the Double Letter numbering sequence was half way through the V combinations. It is noticeable that large numbers of captured German and Italian aircraft carried these registrations. Serials continued post-war and are still current today, having reached the Z range. Interestingly the two British Eurofighter EFA 2000 prototypes are registered ZH588 and ZH590.

Aircraft Codes & Markings :

It should be noted in the squadron and flight histories, official aircraft code lettering is included where known i.e AD- equals No. 60 Squadron. Therefore, it can be stated that an aircrafts unit can be identified by the fuselage code lettering detailed (mostly official WW II designations). In some cases the same coding combination was used by two or more units. As for example, a Hawker Hurricane F.1 displaying AL- could be from No.79 Squadron or No.429 Squadron both of which used AL-code. A check on the aircrafts registration would therefore be required to identify the aircrafts unit.

Bibliography & Sources

Ashworth Chris   Encyclopaedia of Modern Royal Air Force Squadrons. PSL 1989
                            Aviation Magazines & Periodicals. Various
Dancey P   Author - Personal archives
Halley James J.   The Squadrons of the Royal Air Force & Commonwealth 1918 - 1988. Air Britain 1988
Lake Alan   Flying Units Of the RAF.   Airlife 1999
Lewis Peter   Squadron Histories RFC, RNAS, RAF 1912-1959. Putnam 1959
Moyes Philip   Bomber Squadrons of the R.A.F. and their Aircraft. MacDonald 1964
Robertson Bruce   bombing colours. PSL 1972

AIRCRAFT MARKINGS

Fig. 1

Fig. 2

Fig. 3

Fig. 4

AIRCRAFT MARKINGS

Fig. 5

Fig. 6

Fig. 7

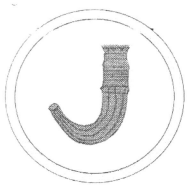

Fig. 8

Fig. 9

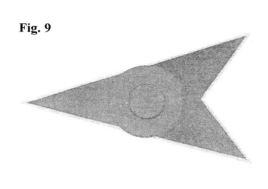

Fig. 10

Fig. 11

Fig. 12

AIRCRAFT MARKINGS

Fig. 14

Fig. 13

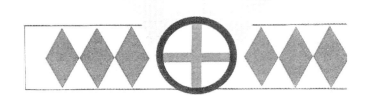

Fig. 15

Fig. 16

AIRCRAFT MARKINGS

Fig. 17

Fig. 18

Fig. 20

Fig. 21

Fig. 19

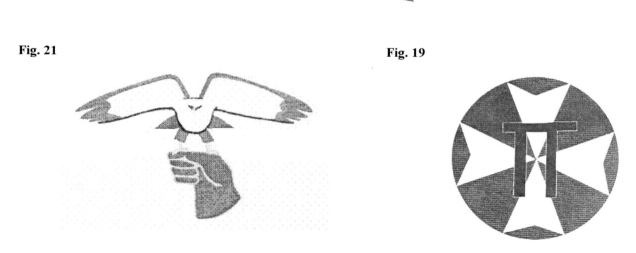

AIRCRAFT MARKINGS

Fig. 22

Fig. 23

Fig. 24

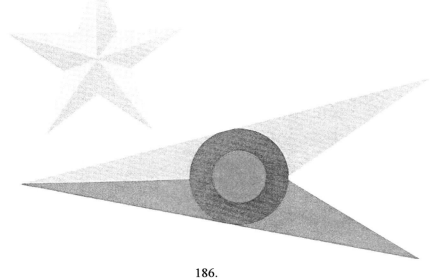

Fig. 25

186.

AIRCRAFT MARKINGS

Fig. 27

Fig. 26

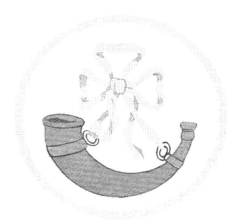

Fig. 28

Fig. 29

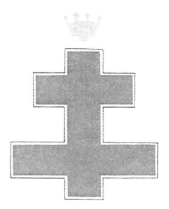

Fig. 30

Fig. 31

Fig. 32

Fig. 33

Fig. 35

Fig. 34

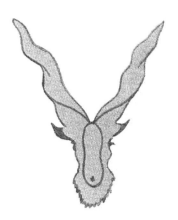

Fig. 36

AIRCRAFT MARKINGS

Fig. 39

Fig. 37

Fig. 40

Fig. 38

Fig. 41

AIRCRAFT MARKINGS

Fig. 42

Fig. 43

Fig. 44

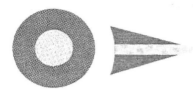

Fig. 45

Fig. 46

Fig. 47

Fig. 48

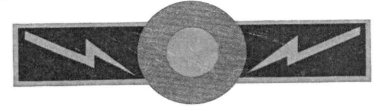

KEY : Aircraft markings

Fig. 1 No 1 (F) Squadron	**Fig. 13** No. 14 Squadron	**Fig. 25** No. 31 Squadron	**Fig. 37** No.74 Squadron (disbanded)
Fig. 2 No. II (AC) Squadron	**Fig. 14** No. 15 Squadron	**Fig. 26** No. 32 Squadron	**Fig. 38** No. 84 Squadron
Fig. 3 No. 3 Squadron	**Fig. 15** No. 16 Squadron	**Fig. 27** No 1 PRU	**Fig. 39** No. 100 Squadron
Fig. 4 No. 4 Squadron	**Fig. 16** No. 17 Squadron	**Fig. 28** No. 33 Squadron	**Fig. 40** No. 101 Squadron
Fig. 5 No. 5 Squadron	**Fig. 17** No. 19 Squadron	**Fig. 29** No. 41 Squadron	**Fig. 41** No. 216 Squadron
Fig. 6 No. 6 Squadron	**Fig. 18** No. 20 Squadron	**Fig. 30** No. 43 Squadron	**Fig. 42** EFTS
Fig. 7 No. 7 Squadron	**Fig. 19** No. 22 Squadron	**Fig. 31** No. 45 Squadron	**Fig. 43** No. 111 Squadron
Fig. 8 No. 8 Squadron	**Fig. 20** No. 23 Squadron	**Fig. 32** No. 51 Squadron	**Fig. 44** No. 208 Squadron
Fig. 9 No. 9 Squadron	**Fig. 21** No. 25 Squadron	**Fig. 33** No. 54 Squadron	**Fig. 45** No. 4 FTS
Fig. 10 No. 11 Squadron	**Fig. 22** No. 27 Squadron	**Fig. 34** No. 60 Squadron	**Fig. 46** No. 202 Squadron
Fig. 11 No. 12 Squadron	**Fig. 23** No. 28 Squadron	**Fig.35** No.64 Squadron (disbanded)	**Fig. 47** No. 230 Squadron
Fig. 12 No. 13 Squadron	**Fig. 24** No. 29 Squadron	**Fig.36** No.65 Squadron (disbanded)	**Fig. 48** No. 617 Squadron

Notes